COLONIAL SETTLEMENTS IN AMERICA

Jamestown
New Amsterdam
Philadelphia
Plymouth
St. Augustine
Santa Fe
Williamsburg
Yerba Buena

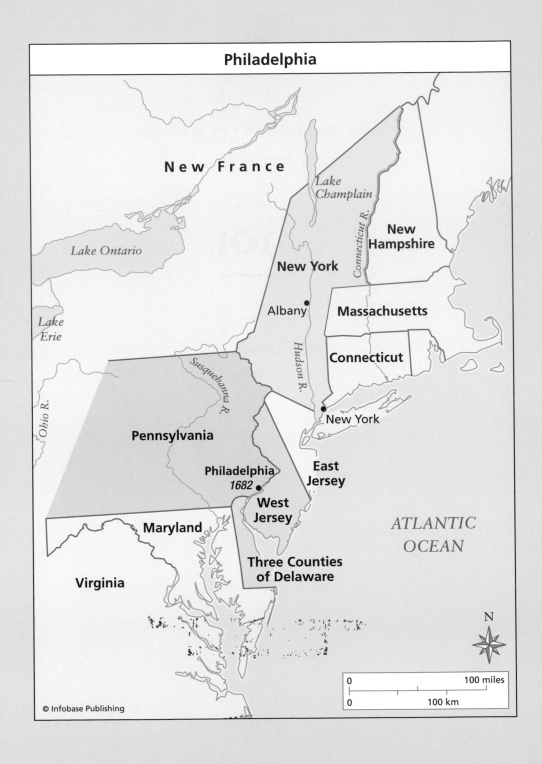

Philadelphia

New France

Lake Ontario

Lake Erie

Lake Champlain

Connecticut R.

New York

New Hampshire

Albany

Massachusetts

Hudson R.

Connecticut

Susquehanna R.

Ohio R.

Pennsylvania

New York

East Jersey

Philadelphia
1682

West Jersey

Maryland

Virginia

Three Counties of Delaware

ATLANTIC OCEAN

N

| 0 | 100 miles |
| 0 | 100 km |

© Infobase Publishing

COLONIAL SETTLEMENTS
IN AMERICA

Plymouth

Tim McNeese

CHELSEA HOUSE
PUBLISHERS
An imprint of Infobase Publishing

Contents

1

Under Siege

Fifty or sixty Englishmen and women gathered in the chapel of the old manor house in "the mean townlet of Scrooby."[1] The small town of Scrooby was located in northern England, less than 50 miles south of the larger English community of York. The great English capital of London was located another 184 miles south of Scrooby. Scrooby was on the great road between London and Edinburgh, far to the north, in Scotland. Nearby Scrooby was the legendary Sherwood Forest, the haunt of the fictional Robin Hood and his Merry Men. It was the fall of 1606. The members of this small Christian group came together for their weekly worship in the chapel of the "great manor-place, standing within a moat."[2]

A HOUSE FILLED WITH HISTORY

The manor house the group gathered in had already been touched by the pages of English history. More than a century earlier, in June 1503, King Henry VII's daughter Margaret had spent the night at the manor house while passing through the

One of the prominent figures among the early dissenters to the Church of England was William Brewster. In 1606, Brewster helped establish the Separatist Church of Scrooby, which believed that the foundation of the church was God's Spirit, rather than the Anglican belief that the state and religious leaders controlled the church.

region. She had just been married to King James IV of Scotland and traveled through Scrooby on her way to her new home in Scotland. Almost 40 years later, in 1541, King Henry VIII also had stayed a night at the Scrooby manor house. Now, the manor house was the home and station of the local postmaster, William Brewster, who was among those who gathered there to worship. (His father, also named William, had been postmaster before him, having moved his family, including his five-year-old son, to Scrooby in 1571.) He was already an important leader among the Scrooby Christians. He would be even more important when they decided to sail to America in 1620.

This small gathering of Christians had recently made an important decision. As English subjects, they had been taught to be loyal to the English king and be faithful members of the king's church, the Church of England, or Anglican Church. But these Christians were driven by their view of their religion to reject the official church organization. They had decided that the Church of England did not represent the true body of believers. They had determined that the Church of England taught many beliefs the Scrooby Christians could not accept. They wanted the Church of England to reform, to change its structure and some of its religious ideas. They wanted the official English church to become less like the Catholic Church, whose doctrines the Scrooby Christians also did not like. In their preaching and teaching, Christians such as those at Scrooby wanted to bring about these changes in the Church of England. Seeking to "purify" the church, these Christians were sometimes called *Puritans*. On that autumn day in 1606, the decision to separate from the Church of England was made one person at a time. It appears that "there was first one who stood up and made a covenant, and then another, and these two joined together, and so a third, and these became a church."[3]

SEPARATED BY FAITH

To that end, the Scrooby sect of Puritans had officially separated from the Church of England. And they were not alone. In another village, Austerfield, just two miles to the north, lived another Puritan convert, William Bradford. Like Brewster, he would one day play an important role in establishing a Puritan colony in America. He would be the governor of Plymouth

Colony. A third village, Gainsborough, was situated 10 miles east of Scrooby. The Puritan movement may have originated there in 1602. The group had begun quietly, with Brewster and Bradford as two of its original members. In those early days of the Puritans, Brewster and Bradford had traveled "every Sunday, on foot from Scrooby and Austerfield,"[4] to join their brethren in Gainsborough to worship and hear the preaching of their minister, John Smyth.

These Puritan Christians at Scrooby, as well as those at Gainsborough and Austerfield, could be described as simple English folk. They lived in a region that was known for its agriculture, and the vast majority of them were farmers—poor farmers, at that. Many of them did not own land, but worked the fields controlled by the archbishop of York. While it appears that nearly all of them were literate, they were not highly educated people. Only a handful of the Puritan group—Brewster, Bradford, and perhaps one or two others—could be considered well educated. On the whole, these Puritans were honest, hardworking souls who held strong beliefs and convictions.

In its earlier days, the church established by the Puritans at Gainsborough had not chosen to criticize the Church of England. Its members even continued to attend the state church's worship services. They had no minister of their own or official teacher or even a written theology different from that of the Church of England. During their first year, they met very informally, sometimes on Sunday afternoons or at other times during the week. Only later did they begin meeting on Sunday mornings. Still, they did not have their own preacher, only those who agreed to come and deliver an occasional sermon. Such visiting preachers were often paid, it appears, out of Brewster's pocket. But by the autumn of 1606, the separation from the Church of England was made, and the Puritans at Scrooby established the Plymouth Church, with Brewster as their chosen leader. Soon,

Located in central England's Nottinghamshire County, the Scrooby manor house was the home of William Brewster and served as the gathering place for the Scrooby Christians. Because they were dissenters, the Scrooby group was forced to hold their weekly religious meetings in private.

however, Bradford left the Gainsborough congregation and began worshipping at Scrooby. (He simply found that the walk was shorter from Austerfield to Scrooby than from Austerfield to Gainsborough.)

Meetings among the Scrooby Puritans were often held in the hayloft of the manor house stable. Their meetings often included prayer sessions and sharing their religious thoughts with one another. To avoid the watchful eye of Anglican authorities, the Plymouth Church usually met in secret. It was thought to be a matter of life and death. Government officials were known to break into such Separatist meetings. They even broke into the homes of the Separatists, looking for religious books and other materials that were illegal to own in Anglican England. Some dissenters were rounded up, taken to prison, and left there. If there was a trial, it might be years before it took place. Some members had their tongues pierced with hot irons or had an ear cut off. No one was safe. Officials would arrest anyone, young and old alike, people whose only crime was worshipping as they thought best, and put them in dingy dungeons where death was common.

A FAITH CHALLENGED

Although members of the Scrooby church met quietly and in a low-key manner, the new congregation had not been established for long before its members were facing challenges from the outside. Initially, it did not come from high officials in the Church of England in York. The archbishop of York knew of the Puritan movement, but he let them practice in peace. Scrooby was a little place, after all, out of the way, and, besides, the archbishop reasoned, why should he "interfere with so peaceable a congregation"?[5]

However, after a year of meeting, the Scrooby group found itself under investigation by Church of England officials in York. The Anglican leaders had received many complaints from parishioners that the Puritans were meeting in defiance of the state church. In November 1607, five members of the Scrooby church, including William Brewster, were summoned before Anglican officials. Four of the five escaped before being taken into custody. Although Brewster avoided capture, his wife did not. She was arrested and held in York Castle. The fifth, a member named Gervase Neville, was arrested and accused of teaching ideas different from those held by the Church of England. Authorities threw him into the York Castle jail. (After testifying on his own behalf, Neville was eventually released after serving some time in jail.) Other Puritans were soon targeted. William Bradford, writing later, explained how some among his number

William Bradford, who later served as governor of Plymouth
Colony for all but five years from 1621 to 1656, joined
William Brewster as one of the early Christian Separatists.
Although they initially practiced their religion in England,
by 1608, the Separatists had been forced to flee England and
move to Holland.

were hunted and persecuted on every side, so as their former
afflictions were as flea-bitings in comparison of those which
now came upon them. For some were taken and clapt up in
prison, others had their houses besett and watcht night and
day, and hardly escaped their hands; and the most were faine
to flie and leave their howses and habitations and the means
of their livelehood.[6]

The Plymouth Church Puritans were finding themselves under siege. But what to do? They were Englishmen and women. England was their home, as it had been for their families for generations. Could the Puritans ever bring about change within the Church of England? Some thought not. They began considering uprooting themselves from their native land and leaving. But where to go? Where could they find peace and practice their faith without interference or threat? Some believed the answer lay in another part of Europe, where religious freedom was the law of the land. In time, the Puritans at Scrooby looked to another place, riskier perhaps, but a place of great possibilities for those who believed God would bless them no matter where they settled.

2

The Decision

Ironically, it was the creation of the Church of England by King Henry VIII that helped in the establishment of the religious sect that had first called its members *Puritans* in 1605. The story begins in the previous century, when, in 1534, the Catholic Church in England was separated from the pope and the main body of the Catholic Church by King Henry VIII. Henry, for both personal and national reasons (he had been denied a writ of divorce from an earlier pope), allowed the development of a separate Christian church, which would come to be known as the Church of England. By rejecting the power of the pope over Christians in England, Henry VIII had established himself as the head of his newly separated church body.

BREAKING AWAY FROM THE CHURCH

King Henry's move away from the Catholic Church was not the only one of its kind in the sixteenth century. Earlier in the 1500s, a movement had begun to form in defiance of the Catholic Church and especially the Italian-controlled papacy.

In the early 1500s, German theologian Martin Luther (1483–1546) confronted the Catholic Church for its corruption. Luther's 95 Theses, which he wrote in 1517, challenged the Church's teaching on the nature of penance, and thanks to the newly invented printing press, his theses quickly spread throughout Europe.

Led by a German theologian and university professor, Martin Luther, the movement protested the teachings and corruptions of the Catholic Church and promoted the view that individual Christians could study the Bible and discover the truth of God's will on their own. They did not need a priest or other Catholic religious leader to tell them how to seek salvation or find God's grace. These free-thinking Christians soon became known as Protestants. All across Europe, the movement spread; although it took root differently across the continent. After all, everyone was free to think for themselves concerning their religion and their faith. Quickly, the Protestant movement fanned out in several directions.

In England, following the death of King Henry VIII, his daughter Elizabeth I rose to the throne and continued the struggle against the Catholic Church in England. She naturally supported the directives of the Church of England, even as she fought Catholicism. In part, to that end, she listened to the various Protestant groups that had sprung up throughout England as they called for the Church of England to eliminate all of its remaining Catholic rituals and practices. In 1563, she called a meeting of churchmen to consider a list of 39 changes for the Church of England that would guarantee the religious body would remain "Protestant in form and rite."[7] This meeting of theologians called for changes that included rejecting the Catholic concept of transubstantiation (this is the belief that the wine and bread of the Communion, or Eucharist, become the actual body and blood of Jesus) and the adoption of the Protestant doctrine of predestination.

But these changes in the Church of England did not satisfy the early Puritans. Just a few years later, a Puritan pamphlet was issued, titled *Admonition to Parliament* (1572). The work argued that the Church of England was not different enough from the Catholic Church. Then, a well-educated Puritan minister named Robert Brown spoke out, going even further. He called for complete separation from the Church of England. Those who agreed with and followed him became known either as Brownists or Separatists.

Other groups of English dissenters remained Puritans. The Puritans had become part of the Protestant movement. In the

In 1607, the Puritans met with King James I to request that the Church of England be reformed. Unfortunately for the Puritans, James favored the "divine right of kings" and forced William Brewster to move his group of Christian Separatists to Holland, where they could freely practice their religion.

beginning, the Puritans hoped to bring about changes in the Church of England one day, especially to make it less formal, a body not requiring a priesthood. Not only did the Puritans desire less formality in their church structures, they also wanted

CLYFTON AND ROBINSON:
THE TWO OTHER PURITAN LEADERS

No other two men were more important to the early seventeenth-century Puritan movement in Scrooby than William Brewster and William Bradford. Their leadership among those of the Scrooby congregation would prove crucial, not only in England, but in the New World colony of Plymouth, as well.

But Bradford and Brewster were not the only important leaders of the early Puritans in Scrooby. Two additional names must be added to the short list of those who made important contributions to the movement—Reverends Richard Clyfton and John Robinson.

Richard Clyfton was one of the few in the group who was highly educated. Just as Brewster had been, Clyfton was educated at Cambridge, one of the leading English universities of that day. Before joining the Scrooby movement, Clyfton had served as the rector of the English Church in Babworth, a small village located about eight miles south of Scrooby. Even though he was an Anglican official, Clyfton became concerned with several scandals that took place among some of the leaders of the Church of England in the region.

One such official, the Bishop of Lichfield, was accused of taking bribes from local craftsmen, including some tailors and shoemakers, to declare them church ministers. (As ministers, these men would have received payments of support from the Church of England.) Clyfton was appalled by such behavior on the part of his fellow churchmen and left the Church of England to become a Puritan. When the church was established in Scrooby, Clyfton became its first official pastor.

His ministerial assistant was John Robinson. He came to the Scrooby church after Clyfton, probably in 1604. Like Brewster and Clyfton, Robinson was educated at Cambridge. Early in his career, he was appointed to lead a parish near Norwich. But he changed his views of the Church of England and eventually became a critic of the Anglican Church. When he left the state church, he, too, joined the Scrooby movement.

to lead their lives in a more simple way, free from the challenges, distractions, and temptations of the world around them. As a result, the Puritans became known for their strict teachings and strong, narrow morality. They came to believe that such practices as dancing or going to the theater would lead one to sin. Instead, the Puritans stayed away from vices that were otherwise common.

One myth about the Puritans is still commonly believed. But unlike the stereotype, the Puritans did not always wear drab, black-and-white clothing. They enjoyed color, and their clothing often featured deep shades of orange, red, blue, yellow, purple, and brown, in hues they called the "sadd colors." They were, however, opposed to wearing flashy, gaudy, or elaborate clothing that made someone stand out as if he or she were more important or wanted to be noticed.

The Puritans filled their lives with hard, honest work. Such work, they believed and taught, would keep one pure from the world and provide all the happiness and contentment he or she might possibly need. As one Puritan leader described his brethren: "Their desires were sett on the ways of God and to enjoye his ordinances."[8]

PERSECUTION AND DECISION

And now the Puritans in England were being persecuted for these and other beliefs. The king's agents and soldiers were scouting the countryside for Puritan meetinghouses and for their outspoken leaders. As for William Brewster, authorities were having a difficult time finding him and for good reason. Brewster had fled the region and gone to the Lincolnshire port town of Boston. There he busied himself making arrangements for him and his congregation to leave England. After all, the Gainsborough congregation, along with their minister, John Smyth, had already left for Holland two years earlier. In this country of the Dutch, everyone was free to practice his or her religion as he or she saw fit. Brewster had heard good reports from Smyth's party, who told him they had found, in Holland, "spiritual comfort and a congenial environment."[9] It appears that Brewster and his group made the decision to flee England sometime in the spring or early summer of 1607.

Preparations for the trip would be simple. These Puritans had little of any worth; only a few of them owned any property or even a house. They were nearly all tenant farmers. Those who had property liquidated their holdings for cash, including Brewster. The remainder of their humble belongings—books, clothes, household items—they packed for the journey. Although the exact number of Scrooby Puritans who chose to move to Holland is not known, it is estimated that the party may have included about 100. When the time came to leave their homeland, English law was not on their side. Legally, they were not allowed to leave with their belongings and money if they had no intention of returning to England. Given those circumstances, the Puritan exiles chose to leave England without any official permission. These Puritan Christians, who valued their strong morality, were forced to take flight for Holland like "criminals or conspirators."[10] No longer were the Scrooby Christians going to call themselves Puritans. They were giving up on "purifying" the Church of England. They were leaving the country of their birth and becoming Separatists.

ESCAPE TO HOLLAND

To leave England quietly and illegally, the members of the Scrooby congregation had to plan well. It was September 1607. The men probably walked to Boston in small groups at night to avoid being seen. The women and children were taken, along with each family's belongings, down the local rivers—the Trent and the Humber—in small boats to the Boston docks. The "escape" plan centered on Brewster having hired a shipmaster who would sail the group of religious dissenters and their household goods to Holland. Once they all arrived at Boston, the group remained out of sight until the shipmaster came to them one night to get them to board his ship and make for open water. The excited Scrooby Christians were soon disappointed, however, when the captain chose to turn them in to the local customs officers.

The port officials searched them thoroughly, then marched them through the town marketplace, humiliating them, "a spectacle and wonder to the multitude which came flocking on all sides to behould them."[11] The unfortunate Separatists were taken to the Boston Guild Hall and placed in cells in the building's cellar. Fortunately, the local magistrates were sympathetic to them and tried to treat them as well as possible. They even had them taken from their cells and confined in more comfortable private homes in the town. But the Separatists had to wait while word was sent to the London Privy Council, who advised the king. What should be done with these English citizens who were trying to leave the country illegally? Finally, after a month of anxious waiting, the answer came back from London. The high authorities were not interested in this small group of Separatists. The majority were released. But seven of their leaders, including William Brewster, were held for trial.

3

A New Home

The arrest of William Brewster raised concern for the Puritans of Scrooby. He and several other Puritan leaders were to stand trial. But these fears were soon put to rest. No hearing was ever held as far as the historical record reveals, and Brewster and the others were allowed to go free. Over the next several months, the Scrooby Separatists managed to make their way to Holland in various ways and in smaller groups. In the details, there is little information. Some appear to have left England that fall and reached the Netherlands before the end of the year. Another attempt to leave England was made by several others in the spring of 1608. Bradford and Brewster were among them. This time, the Separatists had made arrangements to sail on a Dutch ship. They chose to meet the Dutch vessel at a remote location along the English shore, away from any important port. But, again, things did not go well for the would-be exiles.

THWARTED PLANS

The party reached the rendezvous spot a day early, and the women and children, who had again floated down a river to the coast, had to ride out the day in coastal waters that churned and rolled, making many of the women seasick. The next day, the Dutch ship arrived. Hurriedly, the ship's captain took the men onboard. Just then, "a numerous and motley crowd from the country side, some on horseback, most on foot, some with muskets and some with older weapons,"[12] approached the Dutch vessel. This "posse" included local officials from the closest town, as well as soldiers, who had heard of the Separatists' illegal departure. Suddenly, the Dutch captain ordered his crew to take the ship out to sea, leaving the women, along with both Bradford and Brewster, on the shore and under arrest. A second attempt to leave England was falling apart. The women "melted in teares seeing their poore little ones hanging aboute them crying for feare and quaking with [cold]."[13]

The Dutch ship carrying the men of the religious party continued on to Holland. Their voyage would be a rocky one, for their ship was battered by a giant storm that blew in across the North Sea. For two weeks, their ship was driven in every direction by the high winds and relentless rains. The Dutch vessel bobbed about on a dark sea through the storm, for "they saw neither sun, moon, nor stars," for an entire week.[14] The ship became lost at sea because the captain could not take accurate readings on his crude instruments to locate his bearings. The storm was so severe that even the ship's seasoned crew became afraid and "with shrieks and cries, declared that the ship was sinking."[15] As Bradford would later tell the story, the Separatist men dropped to their knees and earnestly prayed that the ship would make it through the storm and find a safe harbor. Finally the storm broke, and the Dutch vessel found its way to Amsterdam, where they thanked God for delivering them from the tempest that had nearly capsized their ship.

Those who were left behind in England were once again brought before local judges. These officials, however, did not know exactly what to do with them. The religious dissenters were shuffled around from one justice of the peace to another, with each choosing to do little or nothing. In time, they were released with a warning to return to their homes and remain there. But no one kept an eye on them and the Separatists remained determined to leave England for the refuge of Holland. In small groups, they did just that over the following six months. The details of their various sailings are largely unrecorded, but it appears the last of them reached the Netherlands in August 1608, nearly a year after they had first intended to make their way out of England. On the last ship to arrive in Holland were Brewster and Bradford, who had remained behind to ensure that everyone made it safely out of England.

A NEW WORLD AMONG THE DUTCH

In Holland, these English Separatists found themselves living in a whole new world. The city of Amsterdam was a prosperous community, a bustling business center where the economy was driven by an expanding trade in herring, as well as a booming cloth industry. Dutch ships came and went from the local port in large numbers, bound for trade ports on the far side of the world. Goods came into Amsterdam from Asia and the Caribbean islands of the West Indies. There were jobs in Amsterdam, something the Separatists had worried about before leaving their English farms. All throughout the city, there was a great demand for unskilled workers. The Pilgrims, for they were on a religious journey that would not soon end, had landed in the right place for work, as "nowhere in Europe was there at that time a community in which a hundred pairs of hands could be more quickly or easily put to work."[16]

However, the Pilgrims stayed in Amsterdam less than a year. Although they could find work, the city was a distraction to them. It was filled with other religious groups who had come for the same reason the English Separatists had come—religious freedom. The city was "the Fair of all the Sects where all the Pedlars of Religion have leave to vend their Toyes."[17] There were Christians of every denomination—Anabaptists, Arians, Unitarians, the homegrown Dutch Reformed Church—as well as Jews. The Puritans considered these groups just as dangerous as the Anglicans and Catholics they had left behind in England. There were distractions of another sort, as well. The local Dutch enjoyed many activities that the Pilgrims did not approve of, including gambling and other vices. The taverns of the city remained open even on Sundays. And there was another problem. The Scrooby congregation soon became involved in a disagreement with the congregation of English Separatists from Gainsborough, those who had fled to Holland a few years earlier. The "flames of contention" spread until "no means they could use would doe any good to cure the same."[18] For all these reasons, the members of the Scrooby church decided to leave Amsterdam and establish themselves in another Dutch community. After much debate, they chose Leyden, a city of 50,000 residents. Before moving, the Puritan group delivered a letter to city authorities on February 12, 1609, asking permission to move to Leyden. Permission was granted the following May. One attraction for the Separatists was the fame of the town's university. Like Amsterdam, Leyden was known for its cloth manufacture, but it was a smaller city. It was also appealing in another way for the Puritans: There were almost no other dissenter groups in Leyden.

Leyden became a true home to 100 or so Scrooby Puritans. When they arrived, they began seeking jobs. Holland in the early seventeenth century was not known for its extensive agriculture. Many people worked by tending livestock and in manufacturing. With few farming jobs available, the Puritans took work in

During the Puritans' stay in Holland, they were joined by Miles Standish, a professional soldier who at the time was fighting in the Low Countries (present-day Holland, Belgium, and Luxembourg). In 1620, Standish and his wife, Rose, sailed with the Pilgrims to America, where he became the military advisor for Plymouth Colony.

manufacturing. Some became weavers, working with different fabrics, such as wool, linen, silk, fustian, and cotton—although cotton was rare at that time. (Fustian was a coarse, durable cloth, a blend of cotton and flax. William Bradford himself became a

(continues on page 30)

CAPTAIN JOHN SMITH
AND THE PILGRIMS

History remembers Captain John Smith as one of the most important men who founded the English settlement at Jamestown in Virginia in 1607. He served as the early settlement's military expert, one who had fought in wars around the world during his early twenties. Although Smith only remained in Jamestown for three years (he was badly wounded in an accidental gunpowder explosion in 1610), no one did more to keep the settlement going than he did.

But Smith should also be remembered for the secondhand contribution he made to the establishment of the Pilgrim colony in New England in 1620. A few years after his gunpowder accident, Smith wanted to return to America. He had fallen out of favor with the officials in charge of the Jamestown settlement, however. So, in 1614, he signed on to captain a whaling fleet bound for America. The fleet sailed across the Atlantic, reaching lands several hundred miles north of Jamestown, a region Captain Smith would name New England. As the whalers searched for their prey, Smith busied himself exploring the region, drawing careful maps. He spent much of his time checking out the river mouths and estuaries along the southern coast of modern-day Massachusetts. The region looked inviting to him, and Smith believed that it would serve as a good site for a colony.

When he returned to England, Smith wrote a small book on what he had seen in New England and promoted the region for colonization. In his *Description of New England*, published in 1617, Captain Smith described the region:

> . . . planted with gardens and corn fields, and so well inhabited with a goodly, strong and well proportioned people [the Native Americans] besides the greatness of the timber growing on them, the greatness of the fish and the moderate temper of the year . . . Who can but approve this a most excellent place, both for health and fertility? And of all the foure parts of the world that I have yet seene not inhabited, could I have but meanes to transport a colonie, I would rather live here than any where.*

It would be Captain Smith's description of New England that would inspire colonists, including the Brownists. William Brewster obtained a copy of the book and read it over and over with great enthusiasm. William Bradford also read the book. By the time they read Smith's work, these

Although John Smith is better known for his exploits at the Jamestown settlement in Virginia, he sailed to New England in 1614 to map the region from Penobscot Bay to Cape Cod. Upon his return to England, Smith wrote *A Description of New England*, which promoted the region for colonization.

Puritan leaders were living in Holland along with other Scrooby exiles. By then, the group was looking for another place to establish their religious community. To them, based on Smith's words and descriptions, New England appeared to be just the right place. Within a few years, the Pilgrims headed for the New World and would establish their colony along a portion of the Massachusetts coast, where Smith had said a colony should be built.

* Peter Charles Hoffer, *The Brave New World: A History of Early America* (Boston: Houghton Mifflin Company, 2000), 181.

(*continued from page 27*)
fustian worker in Leyden.) As for Brewster, he took a position as an English tutor to the sons of several wealthy Dutch families. Reverend Robinson served as the congregation's minister. Richard Clyfton, who was elderly, chose to remain in Amsterdam.

Life in Leyden was satisfactory to the Separatists from Scrooby. Although many of them worked, they were typically poor. Yet they became known for their upright morals and disciplined lifestyles. They had such a reputation for honesty that the local Dutch merchants willingly offered them credit, despite their poverty. The Puritans, it appears, paid their debts. The congregation also became known for its strong fellowship and ability to get along with one another. After a decade in Leyden, the city officials noted that the Scrooby Christians "never had any suit or accusation against any of them."[19]

Perhaps because of their good reputation, the group attracted some converts. Several were Englishmen living in the city. One was Edward Winslow, who would later be chosen three times as governor of the New England Plymouth Colony. Another was John Carver, who would serve as the colony's first governor. There was a soldier, Miles Standish, who would be tapped as the military leader of the Plymouth group.

THEIR HOLLAND HOME

For 12 years, the Puritans called Holland their home. However, even though life in Leyden remained acceptable in some ways to the Scrooby Brownists, with each passing year, many in the group became dissatisfied with life in Holland. They wanted to live in a place where they could practice their religion freely, but they were concerned that their children were growing up speaking Dutch. Some of the Dutch social customs were unacceptable to the Puritans. There were other reasons for dissatisfaction. Bradford himself wrote later on the subject, listing three reasons why the group would eventually choose to leave

Holland for another place of sanctuary. One was the continuing difficulty of life in a foreign country. The Puritans had been forced to take jobs that were new to them. The work they did was often monotonous. (Sometimes when new English Puritans reached Leyden, they did not stay for this very reason.) Another reason was that the Separatists became concerned that their children was forced to work to supplement the family incomes. The effect, according to Brewster, was that the Puritan children "appeared to be growing old before their time."[20] Finally, not only were there moral issues with living among the Dutch, but the children of the Scrooby group were beginning to marry the children of their Dutch neighbors. Since the Puritans were such a small minority group, they feared that, if they remained in Holland much longer, they would simply become part of the general Dutch population, and all that was English about them would one day disappear. (By 1620, 33 members of the Leyden congregation had already become Dutch citizens.) For the Separatists at Leyden, history was to repeat itself. They were going to leave yet another country because of their faith.

4

The Mayflower

Even as the Separatists in Leyden made their decision to leave
Holland, they were not certain of the place they would next call
home. The first serious discussions on the subject had taken
place during the winter of 1616–17. Several places were considered. Many in the Leyden congregation wanted to sail to America and build a religious settlement in the English colony of Brit-
ish Guiana in South America. The weather was always favorable
to farming, and the land was rich and fertile. Others suggested
the English settlement in Virginia—Jamestown—that had been
established in 1607, just before the Separatists had made their
own way to Holland.

PLANS FOR A COLONY

Talk of these places in the Americas frightened many of the
group's members. They knew the stories of starvation at
Jamestown and how it had led to cannibalism among the English colonists. There were stories among them of the cruelty
of the New World Indians, whom some claimed "flayed men
with the shells of fishes, and cut off steaks and chops, which

they then broiled upon the coals before the victim's eyes."[21] Such a move to the New World would be expensive, others noted, an important point considering the relative poverty of many of the Leyden group. Some argued that such a move could prove disastrous for their members. Perhaps, they said, it would be better to remain in Holland or even to return to England than to take on the risks that could be found on the frontier of English colonial America.

In time, the decision was made to attempt to build a colony in North America, perhaps close to Jamestown, but not so close that the Englishmen there could actively persecute them for their religious beliefs. The group selected two of their members, John Carver and Robert Cushman, to travel to London and try to get permission for a Separatist colony in the New World. Their connection in London would be Sir Edwin Sandys.

Sir Sandys's father had been archbishop of York in earlier years, when both the elder and the younger William Brewsters had been the Scrooby postmasters. Perhaps the younger Sandys and the younger Brewster had known one another as boys. At least Edwin Sandys knew of Brewster as an adult and thought well of him. Sandys was also sympathetic to Puritanism. He was an important member of the London branch of the Virginia Company, the joint-stock company that had established the Jamestown settlement in the New World. The Virginia Company had two branches: the Virginia Company of London and the Virginia Company of Plymouth. Each had its own land grant that had been issued by the English Crown. The Plymouth Company's land grant ran from modern-day Maine south to the Potomac River in Virginia. The London Company's grant extended from the mouth of the Hudson River (where New York City would one day stand) south to modern-day North Carolina. The two land grants overlapped between the Hudson River and the Potomac River. When Carver and Cushman met

Sir Edwin Sandys was the son of Edwin Sandys, who served as archbishop of York from 1577 to 1588, and his wife, Cicely, both of whom are depicted here. Like his father, Sir Edwin was sympathetic to the Puritan cause and used his influence in Parliament to support the Puritans.

with Sandys, the latter agreed to help them get permission to establish a new English colony in America.

But permission did not come overnight. Carver and Cushman met with members of the Virginia Company first during the summer of 1617. Discussions were still going on 18 months later. Even as late as the spring of 1619, talks between the Separatists and the London Company had not yet reached an end. Then, in May, things changed for the better for the Brownists. Sandys was elected as the treasurer of the Virginia Company, and, by the end of the month, he helped convince company officials to agree to issue a colonial "patent" to the Separatists, which they received in early June. The "patent" was to be located somewhere in the land grant held by the Virginia Company.

PERMISSION GRANTED

The Leyden Separatists now had a land grant in the New World. However, they did not yet have the money to finance such a move from the Old World to the New World. They made several contacts, but nothing panned out. Then, in February or March 1620, a London merchant named Thomas Weston arrived in Leyden with an offer. He was a Puritan himself. He spoke for a group of other London merchants. Weston offered to support the Separatists in their plans for a colony. He proposed a seven-year partnership between his fellow merchants and the Separatists.

The religious colonists were to build a permanent trading post along the Atlantic coast, where they would "trade with the Indians for furs, fish on the Grand Banks, cut lumber in the forests, and perhaps collect sassafras and other rots [roots] then salable in England."[22] The majority of the colonists were to work at these profitable tasks while others built homes, farmed the local fields, and manned the trading post. The colonists were expected to work four days a week for their investors (the term used at the time was *adventurers*) and two days a week for themselves. Through their New World trade and their harvesting of the frontier's natural resources, the London merchants would expect to turn a profit. During the seven-year contract, the houses and other buildings the colonists built would be owned by the merchants, plus all the colony's supplies, food, even their clothes. At the end of the contract, the houses, buildings, and farmlands would become the property of the colonists. It was all quite simple.

But the basic contract arranged between Weston and the Puritans was not acceptable to the London merchants he represented. They looked closely at the contract and saw that they were expected to invest in a group of people who had nothing to offer at the outset. The Separatists were so poor that they had no collateral to offer to cover the merchants' investment if things did not go well in America. Also, they objected to having the colonists gain rights to the houses and other improvements they built in the New World whether a profit had been made by the merchants or not. The London adventurers insisted that such properties be divided or sold between them and the colonists. Also, the merchants did not like the Separatist colonists having two days a week to work for themselves. The adventurers believed that the two days represented "a loophole through which all profit would escape."[23] To entice the merchants to invest in the venture, Weston, alongside Cushman, agreed to change the terms of the agreement. Only then did the merchants agree and begin to provide money and supplies for the proposed colony.

When the Leyden Separatist group received word of the new contract, many of them were disappointed and discontented. Many of them had worked the lands as tenants back in England. They did not want to do the same in America. They saw the agreement as one that turned them into indentured servants. The English colonies in the New World were filled with such workers. They were usually poor people who did not have the money to pay for their own passage to America. Such would-be immigrants agreed to have someone else pay these costs in exchange for labor to pay off the debt. The "indenture" was usually a period of seven years. These immigrants were very restricted by such agreements and, during their seven-year indenture, were not able to get land of their own and establish themselves in America. Single indentured servants were not allowed to marry. This new contract, then, reduced the Separatists to servants of the London merchants. They would not be coming to America as free men and women.

After long discussions and almost constant prayers, the Separatists finally decided in April to send some of their number to establish a New World colony. They had little choice but to accept the harsh terms placed on them by the London adventurers. Only a portion of the Leyden community signed on to go to America. More members decided to remain in Leyden than decided to leave. These first colonists from among their number were meant to be the advance group. Their brothers and sisters would join them at a later date, once the colony had proven successful.

SPEEDWELL AND MAYFLOWER

Sometime during the end of April or perhaps by early May, a small vessel was purchased, the *Speedwell*, and refitted for the Separatists and all their household belongings that they would bring onboard. In the meantime, a second and larger ship, the *Mayflower*, which weighed 180 tons, was being prepared in England at Southampton docks. The Separatists were to sail to the New World on these two vessels.

The day soon arrived when the selected group of Separatists was to leave for Southampton. That day was "spent at [Reverend] Robinson's house and given over to humiliation, fasting, and prayer."[24] On July 21, 1620, the Puritan company set out for Delftshaven, where the *Speedwell* was docked. (Delftshaven is today part of Rotterdam.) They journeyed to the port town along 24 miles of Dutch canals, where they spent their first night in a warehouse along the wharf, "with little sleepe by the most."[25] Everyone was anxious and excited, and the group spent the evening in "friendly entertainment and Christian discourse."[26]

The following morning witnessed a sad separation among the Separatists. Many from Leyden had accompanied their colonist brethren to Delftshaven to see them off. They all went onboard the *Speedwell*, and Reverend Robinson

falling downe on his knees, (and they all with him), with watrie cheeks commended them with most fervente praiers to the Lord and his blessing. And then with mutuall imbrases [embraces] and many tears, they tooke their leaves one of an other; which proved to be the last leave to many of them.[27]

Among those who stayed behind was Reverend Robinson. In fact, he never migrated to the Plymouth Colony.

In time, the coastal tides rose, and the Separatists, now Pilgrims, prepared to set sail. Nearly everyone was in tears, including even a group of Dutch strangers who watched from the dock. The sails were sent up their masts, and the small vessel took to the open sea, a good wind carrying them over the next

ABOUT THE *MAYFLOWER*

Children learn its name early in school. It is, perhaps, the most famous boat in American history. It is the *Mayflower*, the ship that delivered the Pilgrims to America in 1620. Ironically, however, not much is known about the *Mayflower* outside of its famous voyage across the Atlantic in the early seventeenth century.

Historians are not certain what type of ship the *Mayflower* was. Bradford refers to it as "the ship" or "the larger ship" (meaning it was larger than the *Speedwell*) but offers little additional information. From the historical record, some statistics and facts may be pieced together. It was approximately 90 feet long and 24 feet wide, manned by a crew numbering between 15 and 20. The ship had three tall masts. Two—the foremast and the main mast— were rigged with square sails, as was normal. The third mast, called the mizzen mast, featured a triangular lateen sail. Both ends—the aft and fore—had higher decks than the ship's middle deck.

Given its construction, that the *Mayflower* was "broad of beam, short in the waist, low between the decks and in her upper works none too tight,"* the ship was prone to have waves swept across her lower deck. Sailors referred to her as a "wet" ship. The ship sat low in the water, because it was filled with many supplies and more people than it was designed to carry. Despite these limitations, the Pilgrims considered the *Mayflower* to be a seaworthy vessel, one capable of withstanding the challenges of an Atlantic crossing.

The *Mayflower* was not originally designed for many passengers. It had been used earlier as a cargo ship, and since 1616, it had been used four days from their home in Holland to the land they had left years earlier. When they reached Southampton, they found the *Mayflower* was prepared and had been waiting for them for a week. On the docks, a large party of Separatists were also waiting, having come over from London. Some were intent on joining their departing brethren for the New World.

John Weston was also waiting for them, with contracts in hand to be signed by the leaders of the Pilgrim group. Still angered by the lopsided nature of these agreements, there were arguments that resulted in Weston getting angry and leaving the Separatists on their own. The documents had been signed, but

to ship wine from the Mediterranean. In earlier years, the *Mayflower* carried trade goods out of Norway, including fish, timber, turpentine, and tar. Space below the deck was at a premium. The passengers slept in the aft, or rear, of the ship, while the crew had their bunks in the forward section. Between the decks, much of the space was taken up by a shallop, a small boat measuring about 30 feet in length, which was shipped across the Atlantic in pieces to be constructed in the New World. Even though the available sleeping and living space seems limited in today's world, the Pilgrims thought the *Mayflower* to be "sufficiently commodious to prevent any danger from overcrowding."**

Once the *Mayflower* delivered the Pilgrims to New England, the ship remained through the winter, then returned to England. (Captain Christopher Jones died a year later in March 1622.) The ship remained in service until 1624, when, due to its age and poor condition, it was probably broken up and sold for scrap. Nearly 300 years later, the historian J. Rendell Harris published a book on the Mayflower, in which he claimed that a barn in Jordans, England, contained lumber from the old Pilgrim ship. However, there is no clear evidence of this. The barn in question probably does contain the remains of a ship dating from the 1600s, but it may or may not have been the Mayflower.

* Roland G. Usher, *The Pilgrims and Their History* (Williamstown, Mass.: Corner House Publishers, 1977), 70.
** Ibid.

the infuriated Weston stormed away, still owing port dues of 100 pounds on the *Mayflower*. The Pilgrims were uncertain what to do, but eventually decided to sell some kegs of butter, raising the money they needed to have the *Mayflower* clear the port.

READY TO SAIL

In August 1620, the *Mayflower* and the *Speedwell* prepared to set sail from Southampton, England. The Pilgrims, bound for America, and the other passengers onboard the two New World-bound vessels numbered 102. (In addition, there were several dozen crew members.) But who, exactly, were these passengers? The record is not entirely clear. The only three passengers who can be traced back as original members of the Scrooby congregation and residents of Leyden were William Brewster; his wife, Mary; and William Bradford. Among those on these two ships were 38 others who had been members of the Leyden congregation, making the total 17 men, 10 women, and 14 children. The remaining passengers came from England directly. Among them were those who would be important to the new Plymouth Colony, including John Carver, Edward Winslow, Isaac Allerton, Robert Cushman, as well as their families; John Alden; Miles Standish and his wife; and Christopher Martin and William Mullins, two of the adventurers who had helped finance the entire colonizing project (along with their wives, children, and servants). While the Separatists would provide the leadership for the immigrant group, the majority of those who were sailing to America were not part of that religious group. They were "strangers," those who joined the party to find new opportunities of their own in the New World. While they may have had religious differences with the Separatists, they had something else in common with them—they, too, were poor, lower-class Englishmen and women.

This 1847 oil painting by Charles Lucy is entitled *The Departure from Delft Haven*. Reverend John Robinson is depicted here leading the Pilgrims in prayer before they left Holland for America in 1620.

Where in England did the passengers on these two vessels originate from? As it turns out, they came from many regions of England. Twenty-six came from northern England; 46 from eastern England; 27 from southern England; 7 from the Midlands; and 17 from London. Fourteen passengers were from unknown corners of the country. The majority of those on the *Speedwell* and the *Mayflower* came from four English districts, including Norfolk (32), Kent (17), London (17), and Essex (11). These numbers indicate that the majority of the Pilgrims had no connection to the original Scrooby congregation and did not come from northern England either. Adult males accounted for 44 of the group, compared to 19 adult females, and 39 boys and girls. This means that two out of every five passengers on the two ships were children. There were 44 married individuals, including 26 men and 18 women. Bachelor men numbered 26, compared to 1 unmarried woman, a spinster servant. Most of the adults were in their 20s or 30s. Only two were over 50 and nine over 40. Most of these older Pilgrims died during the first year of the colony. As for the important leaders of the group, they were the following ages when the ships left England: Bradford (31), Winslow (25), Allerton (32), Miles Standish (36), John Alden (21).

Problems were the order of the day as the Pilgrims set out from Plymouth bound for America. Once they set out across the Atlantic during the first week of August, they experienced a serious problem with the *Speedwell.* About 300 miles out to sea, the captain of the smaller ship signaled the captain on the *Mayflower,* letting him know that the *Speedwell* was leaking seriously. The ships turned around and returned to England, reaching the port of Dartmouth, where the *Speedwell's* hull was checked top to bottom. After a few minor repairs, the ships set out again, headed west across the Atlantic. After sailing even farther the second time out, a leak again developed, and the ships again returned to England, this time to Plymouth. The leak could not be found. The Pilgrim leaders decided to abandon the *Speedwell* and sail on with only the *Mayflower.* This was a disappointing setback for the Pilgrims. They were reduced to a single ship with everyone crowded onboard, and they had lost valuable time sailing back to England. The leaks onboard the *Speedwell* caused the Pilgrims to lose a month of sea travel time, because the ship did not get underway for a third attempt at its Atlantic sea crossing until September 16.

On September 16, 1620, the *Mayflower* set sail for America from Plymouth, England. One hundred and two colonists, including William Bradford and Miles Standish, made the 66-day voyage across the Atlantic Ocean.

UNDERWAY AT LAST

Little is known about the voyage once the *Mayflower* got underway without the *Speedwell*. On many days, the winds were light and the sea itself relatively calm. Even then, many onboard suffered at least mild cases of seasickness. The trip was not entirely calm, however. About halfway across the Atlantic, violent winds rose and the *Mayflower* sailed into some severe weather. In the midst of a gale that battered the vulnerable, overloaded ship, the *Mayflower's* main beam cracked and slipped out of place. If the damage worsened, the Pilgrim vessel could take on great amounts of water, which would cause the ship to capsize and sink with all passengers lost. The beam had to be repaired. But how? The Pilgrim leaders called a hurried meeting and anxiously discussed their problem. Some panicky passengers were in favor of turning their single ship around a third time and making for the safety of the English coast they had been so anxious to leave behind. Others urged the party to continue the voyage to America and hope for the best.

Then, someone had a good idea. Among the equipment and tools the religious exiles had hauled onboard the *Mayflower* was a large iron jack stored in the ship's hold. The jack's intended use was to help raise the houses the Pilgrims would build in the New World. Men rushed to retrieve the jack. With water seeping through the crack in the ship's beam, the Pilgrims placed the jack under the beam and then screwed it up to put pressure on the main beam. This righted the beam back into place, largely repairing the leak, and correcting the structural damage to the ship. The Pilgrims rejoiced. They had been saved from a storm that threatened their very lives.

The Pilgrims faced other difficulties on their voyage. Living in such close quarters, the passengers found bathing and washing difficult, if not impossible. Another concern was making sure they had enough food. It is known that the immigrants took livestock onboard the *Mayflower,* including goats, pigs, and poultry. These were kept in pens on the forward deck. No cattle were taken, however. Many of these animals were intended for use in the New World, not for consumption on the voyage across. The goats would provide the colonists with milk and cheese, while the birds would provide eggs and the pigs, meat. The bulk of the food brought by the Pilgrims was typical of such a transatlantic voyage, and probably included such staples as dried or smoked meats, such as bacon and salt beef, hard tack (hard biscuits, bread, or crackers), smoked herring, cheese, and beer or ale, both common drinks of the day.

In addition, the Pilgrims larder probably included such "luxuries" as butter, vinegar, mustard, and fruits, perhaps lemons and prunes. There was a quantity of gin and a supply of either brandy or Dutch schnapps. For all their religiosity, the Pilgrims regularly drank alcohol.

The food was doled out to each passenger as a daily ration by leaders, and most of the foods were eaten cold. Cooking on the ship, especially for the number onboard, was difficult at best. The ship was not designed and equipped with a full kitchen, and the cooking that was done was by "a frying pan held over charcoal fire or a kettle suspended on the iron tripod over a box of sand."[28]

The trip across the Atlantic lasted for two months and five days. Its rigors placed special strains on the Pilgrims. One passenger, a young man named William Button, died. From the passenger list that Bradford compiled in a later writing, Button was a servant or apprentice of a Samuell Fuller, who left his wife and child behind when he sailed on the *Mayflower*, intending to bring them over at a later date. Despite Button's death, the *Mayflower* reached the New World with as many passengers as it had taken aboard at Plymouth, England. During the voyage, Stephen and Elizabeth Hopkins had a son, whom they appropriately named Oceanus. Equally appropriate, Oceanus would one day choose seafaring as his life's profession.

THE HIGHLANDS OF CAPE COD

Despite the difficulties experienced by the Pilgrims onboard the *Mayflower*, the passengers finally spotted land on November 9, 1620. That day, the sailors on the ship scanned the coast and immediately identified the region as the highlands of Cape Cod. The cape was a natural barrier, a great flexing arm of land that almost encircled a natural harbor. As Winslow would write: "The bay is . . . round and circling."[29] Jamestown was hundreds of miles to the south. The great storm that the ship had passed through had blown the *Mayflower* off course. While the Pilgrims had not intended to build their colony close to Jamestown, they had probably targeted the mouth of the Hudson River. Now they were north of that landing site.

Disappointed at their destination, the Pilgrims ordered Captain Jones to turn the ship to the south. He did so, and was soon under sail out of the sanctuary of Cape Cod. But soon the ship was in danger, as it "fell amongst dangerous [shoals] and roring breakers, and they [were] so farr intangled therewith, as they conceived themselves in great danger."[30] The shoals in question were probably those of Pollock Rip and the sand spit of Monomoy. Afraid their ship would break up on the rocks, the Pilgrims instructed the ship's captain to return to the relative safety of Cape Cod and its protected harbor. The *Mayflower* returned to the cape and dropped anchor on November 11, a Saturday. Upon this site, the Puritan community of Provincetown would one day be built. The Pilgrims were just glad to have reached America alive. In Bradford's later history, he described how the Pilgrims "fell upon their knees and blessed the God of heaven, who had brought them over the vast and furious ocean and delivered them from all the periles and miseries thereof, again to set their feet on the firme and stable earth, their proper elemente."[31] The Pilgrims had, indeed, survived the perils of the mighty Atlantic Ocean. But they had more challenges ahead of them, and many of their number would not survive.

5

In the New World

With the landing of the *Mayflower* and its precious cargo of religious exiles along the coast of modern-day Massachusetts, rather than its intended destination farther south, much of the future of the Pilgrim colony in the New World had changed. The fact was that the Pilgrims had landed in the wrong place. Nevertheless, the leaders of the colony made an important decision. They decided to remain where they were and not reroute their vessel. But why?

AN IMPORTANT DECISION

The patent, or land grant, given to the Pilgrims who sailed on the *Mayflower* had been given for the building of a colony within the territory that had been granted earlier to the Virginia Company of London. Instead, the newly arrived colonists had reached land that belonged to the Virginia Company of Plymouth. Thus, the Pilgrims had no authority, no permission, no warrant, no legal leg to stand on to establish a colony where they were. Everyone onboard the *Mayflower* knew this to be a fact. But the party decided to remain.

In their writings, the Pilgrim leaders tried to explain their decision to stay in New England. They excused themselves by stating that they had arrived late to the New World and to continue their journey, with the approach of winter, would have been dangerous. Their food supplies were running low. Some of their food had already spoiled. Their flour was full of weevils. They cite Captain Jones's concern about finding a safe haven as quickly as possible, given the lateness of the season. While all of these are good reasons to remain in the vicinity of Cape Cod, there may well be another reason.

The Pilgrims had only grudgingly accepted the terms of the agreement with their London backers to establish their colony in America. The London merchants had placed a heavy burden on the Pilgrims, making them virtual servants who were bound by seven years' service to ensure a profit to the adventurers backing the colony. Under this agreement, the vast majority of the Pilgrims would have had no real rights in their new colony. Remaining in New England would give the colonists the opportunity to strike out on their own. There would be risks, of course. Their colony would not be able to have contact with the colonists at Jamestown. The Pilgrims' colony would be an illegal venture. But they, including their leaders, Bradford and Brewster, were willing to take their chances without having any legal authorization to build their new colony.

This move brought some additional, unexpected problems. Because the colony site was not a legal site, the Pilgrim leaders had no real authority. This view was soon stated clearly by those among their number who were servants or even sailors onboard the ship. The servants saw no reason to take orders or instruction from those who were in charge of a colony that was, in fact, an illegal one. It appeared that, "the abandoning of the original patent would leave every man his own master once the ship

This 1859 painting by American artist Tompkins H. Matteson depicts the signing of the Mayflower Compact in November 1620. The agreement, which was signed by 41 of the male passengers of the *Mayflower*, ensured that the colony was bound by a formal government and that its members would abide by any laws and regulations subsequently established.

had made land."[32] The Pilgrim leaders soon found themselves caught in their own plans. How to keep the colonists united and under their direction became the new goal. And they would have to think of something fast.

THE MAYFLOWER COMPACT

The Pilgrim leaders—including Brewster, Bradford, Winslow, Carver, and Standish—soon came up with a workable solution. They decided to draw up a new agreement. Using the lid of Miles Standish's travel chest as a writing desk, these men drafted a document they would soon call the Mayflower Compact. It was not a lengthy piece of writing, but one of great importance. It not only addressed their difficult situation, it also provided the base for self-government among English colonists in North America. Making their agreement as official as possible, those onboard the *Mayflower* penned a voluntary compact, or contract, that was signed by 41 adult males of the company. It was, of course, worded in the language of the day:

> In ye name of God, Amen. We whose names are underwriten, the loyal subjects of our dread soveraigne Lord, King James, by ye grace of God, of Great Britaine, Franc, & Ireland king, defender of ye faith, &c. Having undertaken, for ye glorie of God, and advancemente of ye Christian faith, and honour of our king & countrie, a voyage to plant ye first colonie in ye Northern parts of Virginia, doe by these presents solemnly and mutually in ye presence of God, and one of another, covenant & combine ourselves together into a civil body politick, for our better ordering & preservation & furtherance of ye ends aforesaid; and by virtue hearof to enacte, constitute, and frame such just & equall lawes, ordinances, acts, constitutions, & offices, from time to time, as shall be thought most mete & convenient for ye generall good of ye Colonie, unto which we promise all due submission and obedience. In witness whereof we have hereunder subscribed our names at Cape-Codd ye. 11 of November, in ye year of ye raigne of our soveraigne lord, King James, of England, France, & Ireland ye eighteenth, and of Scotland ye fiftie fourth. Ano: Dom. 1620.[33]

In writing these words and with their acceptance by nearly all the adult males onboard the *Mayflower*, the Pilgrims made it clear that they had not come to America just to establish a colony where they could worship freely. They had decided to base that colony on local government and control, power accepted by the adult males by their own free choice.

ESTABLISHING THEIR COLONY

Once the Mayflower Compact was drawn up and signed, the Pilgrims put themselves to the work of organizing their colony. One of the first steps they took was to appoint their governor. They selected John Carver to administrate the colony until the next New Year's Day. On the same day as the signing of the Mayflower Compact, the ship put in anchor about a mile from what later became Provincetown. That afternoon, Captain Miles Standish led a party of 16 men, all armed, to go ashore and explore the lands close at hand and return with firewood. It was, after all, winter in New England. (The winter of 1620–21 would be a mild one, however, as well as the following winter.) They were also to scout out a good spot for their settlement. Captain Standish and his men climbed the local sand hills and woods, where they found thick growths of oak, pine, juniper, birch, and holly. They also found abundant sassafras in the region, which excited them. Sassafras root was valuable in England, bringing three shillings a pound. After discovering the lay of the land, Standish and his men soon reported back to the rest of the party.

By Monday, the 13th, the larger group was leaving the *Mayflower* and making for land. They had spent Sunday resting and worshipping. Men began putting the small boat—the shallop—together, which took several days' labor before it was seaworthy. The women took the opportunity to wash clothes in the local ponds while the children enjoyed the freedom of the outdoors, having been cooped up in a ship for more than four months. Other men searched out the land as Captain Standish's party had. Standish and Bradford set out with another group of

(continues on page 54)

THE PILGRIMS AND THE LOCAL NATIVE AMERICANS

One of the early advantages the Pilgrims experienced as they tried to found their colony in the New World was the peace they enjoyed with the local Native Americans. During the first two years the *Mayflower* immigrants were in New England, "the Pilgrims seem to have been in no danger whatever from Indian hostility."* It was not what the Pilgrims had expected before coming to America.

Back in Holland, they had heard stories of how New World natives enjoyed eating human flesh. This proved untrue. Instead, the local tribes loved some of the foods that the Pilgrims brought with them, including buttered biscuits and beer. The real threat to the Pilgrims was that the local natives often made a practice of showing up at Pilgrim settlement sites, expecting to be fed. Hospitality was important to the Native Americans and to turn them down for a meal would have been insulting. The members of one village, located about 15 miles from Plymouth, became known for showing up often and expecting "food, lodging, and diversion."** Sometimes, as many as 50 to 100 people from the same tribe might arrive at Plymouth, all expecting to be fed for two or three days.

In time, the Pilgrims learned about the native groups that were spread out in every direction from Plymouth. The tribes living close to Plymouth belonged to a confederacy called the Wampanoag. Massasoit was their sachem, or leader, and they lived along Narragansett Bay. The group included the small tribes of southeastern Massachusetts and eastern Rhode Island. They had numbered approximately 3,000 warriors before 1617. But a smallpox epidemic, along with several other diseases, had swept through the region between 1617–19, reducing their numbers to about 300. The disease had wiped out the Pawtuxet Indians near Plymouth. As for Massasoit's tribe, it could only boast about 60 warriors.

To the north, near where modern-day Boston would be located, was another Native American alliance, the Massachusetts Confederacy, which included several small tribes. These, too, had been so reduced in numbers by smallpox that the group had only about 100 warriors. With such small numbers, the Massachusetts group allied themselves to Massasoit. Thus, as long as Massasoit was friendly to the Pilgrims, nearly all the local tribes around Plymouth would be, as well.

Two additional confederacies of Native Americans lived in the New England region—the Pequot Confederacy and the Narragansetts—but they were located a good distance from the Plymouth settlement. For that reason, they

From the time the Pilgrims arrived in 1620, the leader of the Wampanoag Confederacy, Massasoit, pursued peaceful relations with the newcomers. Massasoit and his people taught the Pilgrims how to plant crops and helped them get through the first winter at Plymouth.

were never a threat to the Pilgrims. Despite four Indian confederacies in the general area of New England during the early 1600s, the fact is that these Native Americans were "weak in numbers, inferior in development, backward in civilization compared to the Indian tribes of the interior" such as the Iroquois nations of modern-day New York, the Cherokees, or the Creeks.*** Putting all the tribes of the New England region together, their total numbers probably did not add up to as many as 25,000. Whether by providence or sheer luck, the Pilgrims had "stumbled upon a location where the [Indians] were singularly weak, disorganized, and inferior in quality even for the Indians of the coast."†

---

* Quoted in Roland G. Usher, *The Pilgrims and Their History* (Williamstown, Mass.: Corner House Publishers, 1977), 113.
** Ibid.
*** Ibid., 115.
† Ibid.

(continued from page 51)

men on the 15th and found "traces of game, of Indians . . . and marched up hill and down dale with great toil and fatigue."[34] One problem was the armor. Most of the men were not used to wearing any and its weight wore them down, along with the heavy firearms they carried.

The party found fields that had been cleared by the practice of burning out the forest underbrush to help create natural meadows or cornfields. They discovered an Indian grave, a small hut fashioned out of ship planks and an iron kettle, the latter both signs that other Europeans had reached the same location, as Captain John Smith had. The party also found some hidden supplies of Indian corn, about three or four bushels, which they took. Much of it they saved for seed to plant the following spring. (They paid the Native Americans for it later.)

The Standish group also found fields of red cranberries, a great discovery. Cranberries are rich in vitamin C, which the Pilgrims lacked in their diet. Some of their number were already sick with scurvy, a disease caused by malnutrition and a lack of vitamin C. At one point, the men stumbled along a deer trap made of a bent tree sapling and a noose. Unaware what it was, William Bradford stepped too close, the trap sprung, and he found his leg caught, leaving him swinging in the air. Along the way, the Standish party encountered a group of Native Americans, along with a dog. When they spied Standish's party, they ran away. The group tracked them for several miles, but never saw them again that day.

As the larger party disembarked from the *Mayflower* onto dry land, they knew they were prepared for their New World venture in some ways and not in others. They had brought along many of the supplies they would need. They had a reasonable inventory of cooking utensils, but they were simple items, including pewter or woodenware, as well as metal candle molds and irons for their fires. They had tools for carpentry and blacksmithing, but lacked such things as plows or carts. They did not need such things, because they had no large draught animals. The Pilgrims had planned on fishing and had a good supply of nets and fishhooks. As for protection, the party had brought along guns; swords; a supply of gunpowder; some armor pieces, including breastplates and side armor; and a few cannon.

One of the most urgent problems for the Pilgrims was that of finding food. They had not been able to bring along large supplies of food on the *Mayflower*. They had assumed all along that they would need to trade with the local Native Americans for corn, or maize, to help supplement their food supply. They did bring many items to trade with the local natives. The party also had seed to plant in the spring, for growing onions, turnips, parsnips, cabbages, and carrots. They also had peas and beans.

For the rest of November and through December, the *Mayflower* remained at anchor. It was an important time for the colonists. No other period would prove "more memorable than the five or six weeks passed at Cape Cod."[35] Many of the Pilgrims slept outside without the benefit of tents, something else they had not brought from England. By November 27, the shallop was ready, and another exploration of the region was made, this time by boat. Twenty-four men went along on this trip, with some in the shallop and some in a lifeboat. While they were out, the party was hit by a severe snowstorm. But they continued over the next several days, killing game, including fat geese and a dozen ducks. They found more hidden corn, 10 bushels this time, near the same place they had found corn earlier. This discovery they considered "God's good Providence."[36] The party also named the site Corn Hill.

In the days that followed, the Pilgrim leaders began to consider a spot for their settlement site. Enough exploring of the immediate region had been done, they thought. While several spots were proposed, including Corn Hill, one of the *Mayflower's* sailors, the pilot named Coppin, suggested a good harbor situated a little farther west. The leaders had not explored the site, so they sent a party to check it out. When they returned, they agreed: This harbor site would do well for building the colony. The site would be called Plymouth.

6

Moving to Plymouth

On December 6, a cold day, "so cold that the spray from the oars froze on their clothes and one of their number nearly died of exposure,"[37] the Pilgrims began their move from Cape Cod to Plymouth. The Plymouth site had been occupied previously by Native Americans. There, the colonists found the abandoned village that had been left when a smallpox epidemic struck a few years earlier. The site had definite advantages, including previously cleared land, a freshwater stream nearby, and it was situated on top of a hill that could be easily defended. The move was hampered by cold and rain over the next several days, and the *Mayflower* did not reach Plymouth until December 16, having fought harsh winds.

LIFE AT PLYMOUTH

The arrival at Plymouth marked the beginning of the true colonization of the Pilgrims in the New World. Here they would

When the Pilgrims arrived in America in November 1620, they first landed at present-day Provincetown, on the tip of Cape Cod. Over the course of the next month, they explored the region to find the best place to settle. They eventually chose Plymouth, which is depicted in this lithograph by Currier and Ives entitled *Landing of the Pilgrims at Plymouth Rock in 1620*.

stay and build their unique world as religious settlers on the American frontier. December 17 was a Sunday, and the party was led in worship by Elder Brewster, which undoubtedly included "the singing of psalms, of heartfelt prayers, of the reading of the Scriptures."[38] Brewster's words that Sunday were words of thanks that looked toward the future for the colonists who had finally reached their new home: "May not and ought not the children of these fathers rightly say our fathers were Englishmen which came over this great ocean and were ready to perish in this willdernes but they cried unto the Lord and he heard their voice and looked on their adversitie."[39]

A HARSH REALITY

Life at Plymouth proved difficult. The months that followed the Pilgrims' initial arrival in New England in November were quite cold (despite the winter being milder than normal). Given the cold, the Pilgrim men set about building what shelter they could as fast as possible. (The women generally stayed on the ship to guard against the cold.) The men used their axes to cut down trees and shape them into logs and planks. They had to haul them by hand, because they had no horses or oxen. All this hard work had to be done in freezing temperatures. By January 9, the frame of a Puritan meetinghouse, or "common house," had been completed, measuring 20 feet square. It was a log structure with the spaces between the logs filled with mud. It had a thatched roof, similar to those of Scrooby and Austerfield. But, less than a week later, lookouts on the deck of the *Mayflower* spotted the new building on fire. It had been accidentally set by a match in the house that caught the thatch on fire. Because the tide was out, the Pilgrims could not get to shore to battle the blaze. However, a high wind caused the roof to burn quickly without damaging the roof beams or the building's log frame.

While tragic, the fire could have been worse. No one was hurt in the blaze, even though most of the adult men, including Carver and Bradford, had their beds in the house. There were loaded muskets in the house that fortunately did not discharge. But it was a Sunday, and the Pilgrims did not believe in working on their day of rest. So, the men remained in the house with no roof, while a dreary rain fell on them. The roof was replaced a week later. Construction continued through the following weeks, as small sheds and log cabins were built and thatched. The Pilgrims began unloading some of their supplies from the ship to the colony site. By February 21, the men hauled two cannon ashore and placed them in the hilltop settlement. The Pilgrim village was taking shape.

Entitled *Beginning of New England*, this oil painting by American artist Clyde Osmer DeLand depicts the construction of the first meetinghouse at Plymouth. Throughout their first winter at Plymouth, the Pilgrims battled disease and hunger, and by the end of that winter, more than half of the colonists had died.

Disease continued to ravage their numbers throughout February 1621. William Bradford referred to the condition of his group as the "general sickness," and nearly all members of the group were in poor health. One of the circumstances that led to greater sickness was that both the Provincetown and Plymouth harbors were shallow, causing the *Mayflower* to be anchored far from the actual shoreline, which changed with the tide. The Pilgrims had to wade in and out of water regularly to get to and from the small boats that carried them off and on their ship.

THE STRUGGLE FOR FOOD

Because the party of colonists arrived too late to plant crops, the Pilgrims continued to face regular shortages of food during their first winter. Disease and death stalked the colonists. Without enough food, and given the amount of hard labor they were doing, the Pilgrims began to suffer greatly, weakened by their circumstances. Scurvy ran through the group, as well as pneumonia. William Bradford would later record the dreary circumstances his people had to suffer through during that first New England winter at Plymouth:

> But that which was most sadd and lamentable was that in two or three months' time half of [the] company dyed, especially in January and February, being the depth of winter and wanting houses and other comforts, being infected with the scurvie and other diseases, which this long voyage and their inacomodate condition had brought upon them; so as there dyed sometimes two or three of a day in the aforesaid time, that, of one hundred and odd persons, scarce fifty remained. And of these in the time of most distress there was but six or seven [healthy] persons who, to their great commendations be it spoken, spared no pains, night or day, but with abundance of toyle and hazard of their owne health, fetched them wood, made their fires, drest them meat, made their beds, washed their loathsome cloaths, cloathed and uncloathed them, in a word did all the homely and necessarie offices for them and all this willingly and cheerfully . . . shewing herein their true love unto their friends and brethren.[40]

No one was safe from the chilling hand of death among the Pilgrims at Plymouth. Sadly, the death rate among the mothers of families was extremely high—75 percent. Of 16 women,

(continues on page 64)

A COLONY BUILT ON A ROCK

Over the hundreds of years since their arrival in New England in 1620, the Pilgrims have become the stuff of American legend. Every elementary school student hears stories about the *Mayflower* and the first Thanksgiving. The Pilgrims, in their black-and-white costumes, adorn countless school bulletin boards. Over the years, the story of the Pilgrims has also included an interesting legend—the claim that, when the Puritans reached their new home they would call Plymouth, some of the people, as they disembarked from the *Mayflower* onboard either a lifeboat or the shallop, reached shore and dry land by stepping onto a large rock situated along the coast. In time, it would become known as Plymouth Rock. It is preserved today at Plymouth, encased in a special building and viewed by thousands of visitors each year.

But is the story of Plymouth Rock true? Where did the legend of this rock as a Pilgrim stepping-stone begin? Both the contemporary accounts of the Pilgrims' arrival at Plymouth—Bradford's account and another book, written in 1622—only state that the Pilgrims landed. The rock is not mentioned in either account. In fact, the first references to today's famous Plymouth Rock do not take place until more than a century after the 1620 landing. The story is an interesting one.

Over the decades following the establishment of the Plymouth colony, the story of Plymouth Rock was told again and again. It was passed down orally from one generation to the next. One clear example of this may be seen in the life of Thomas Faunce, who was born in Massachusetts in 1647. His father arrived at Plymouth in 1623 onboard a ship named the *Anne*.

In 1741, when Thomas Faunce was 94 years old, he was well known at Plymouth, where he had served as the presiding elder in the First Church. That year, he was told that a new wharf was to be constructed along the beach that would cover a large rock. He became concerned and asked to be taken to the rock, the site being three miles from his home. A special chair was prepared, and the frail Thomas Faunce was carried to the site. People had heard of Faunce's request and gathered to hear him tell a story that would become part of the legend of Plymouth Rock.

According to Faunce, his father told him that when the Pilgrims landed at Plymouth for the first time, they used the large rock to step out of their boats. Thinking he was seeing Plymouth Rock for the last time, Faunce gave it a farewell as his eyes welled with tears. There were those in the crowd who had heard Faunce's story before. Over the years, he had made annual trips to the rock, where he told his story to his children and grandchildren.

Faunce was certainly a likely source for the truth of such a story. He was nine years old when Miles Standish died, a year older when Bradford died. He had known at least 23 of the *Mayflower* Pilgrims while growing up, and his uncle had been the colony's historian. But there were also other second- and third-generation Plymouth residents who had heard the same story from their relatives and from Faunce himself.

Certainly the story of the Pilgrims landing at Plymouth Rock has remained an important part of their historical record. And efforts have been made to preserve this solid piece of Pilgrim folklore. Those efforts have not always been successful. In 1774, just before the start of the American Revolutionary War, local Plymouth residents tried to remove the rock from the beach to preserve it in a safer place. When they tried to remove it with a team of oxen, the rock broke in two, due to a crack in the stone no one had seen. While the base of the rock was left in place, the upper part, weighing several tons, was placed in front of the town's meetinghouse.

By 1834, the residents of Plymouth decided to move the rock again, this time out in front of Pilgrim Hall. The next year, the local Pilgrim Society enclosed the rock with an elaborate iron fence. The society also began buying up and removing buildings along the wharf near where the base of the rock was located. In 1859, the society laid the cornerstone for a canopy over the rock base along the wharf, which was completed in 1867. In 1880, the group returned the portion of the rock in front of the Pilgrim Hall Museum and placed it on the base, which was shielded by its canopy. Once that move was made, the society had the date "1620" carved into the historical stone.

In 1920, Plymouth, as well as the entire country, celebrated the three hundredth anniversary of the landing of the Pilgrims at Plymouth Rock. That year, the old wharf district was demolished, the whole area landscaped, and the shoreline restructured so that the ancient rock was again at water level. Care over the rock was transferred to the Commonwealth of Massachusetts, and a new pavilion was built over the stone site. Today, the rock still stands as a monument to an important chapter in early American colonial history. The rock visited by tourists is estimated to be about one-third to one-half of its original size. Over the years, the rock shrank as it was removed, dragged across the town of Plymouth, and occasionally broken. It has also been the victim of vandalism, as souvenir hunters have chipped off small pieces to keep as their own personal piece of Plymouth Rock.

In March 1621, the Pilgrims and the Wampanoag Indians, led by Massasoit, agreed to an informal treaty by which each group would provide help and friendship to the other group. The treaty lasted for many decades and did not dissolve until after Massasoit's death in 1661.

(continued from page 61)

12 died that winter. Among the 25 fathers of families (some of them had left their wives in England), 13 became sick and died. Sometimes the members of the group died in such numbers that the living found it difficult to bury them.

HELP FROM THE WAMPANOAGS

During that first winter in Plymouth, half of the Pilgrims died. Among them was Governor Carver. Not long afterward, the Pilgrims chose William Bradford as the colony's new chief magistrate. Bradford would continue as the colony's governor until 1633. That year, he was succeeded by Edward Winslow. Bradford again served as governor from 1635 and 1637, then again in 1639, holding the office for the next five years. After

Winslow served again in 1644, Bradford returned in 1645. He would not step down until 1657. In all, William Bradford served as his colony's governor for a total of 31 years.

But despite its difficult first year, the Plymouth Colony was not doomed to fail, thanks to help the Pilgrims received from local Native Americans, the most important of whom was Massasoit. He was a tribal leader, a sachem, of the Wampanoag Confederacy. Massasoit offered the Pilgrims food, which included Indian corn. But Massasoit wanted something in exchange for helping the English colonists. He wanted them to ally with the Wampanoag against another local tribe, the Narragansett. Relations between Massasoit and the Pilgrims were so positive that, in March 1621, the sachem and the Pilgrim leaders made a "treaty" of sorts, an agreement that each group would provide help and friendship to the other as much as possible. Massasoit's people were not to hurt the Pilgrims, and the Pilgrims were not to injure the sachem's tribe. During the months that followed, various Pilgrim leaders paid visits to Massasoit's village and sat down with him to smoke the ceremonial pipe and share a meal. The Pilgrims offered gifts to the great leader, including a lace-trimmed, red cotton coat, a copper chain, and some smaller trinkets.

SQUANTO'S CONTRIBUTIONS

Another Native American offered invaluable assistance to the Pilgrims. His name was Squanto. The language barrier between the English at Plymouth and the Native Americans of the region would have been much more difficult to overcome without the help of Squanto. Much to the surprise of the Pilgrims, Squanto spoke English! His story is an interesting one. A member of the Pawtuxet tribe, Squanto had just returned to New England a year earlier after having spent several years away. He had been taken on a fishing vessel to England in 1605. There he had lived until 1614, spending several years in London. That year, he was returned to his native land, but a short time later, he was kidnapped again, this time by an English sea captain and sold into slavery in Spain. In time, Squanto escaped and returned to England. By 1619, he was delivered back to New England. When he returned, he was saddened to find his former village had been wiped out by smallpox. Without a tribe or a home, Squanto had joined the Wampanoags. He served as an adviser and interpreter for Massasoit.

Squanto became the most important Native American to the Pilgrims. When, in August 1621, the Pilgrims received word that Squanto had been taken captive by one of Massasoit's own chiefs, one named Corbitant (the story stated he was plotting against Massasoit with the Narragansetts), the Pilgrims immediately decided to go and find their friend, if he was still alive, and "avenge him if he were dead."[41] Ten Pilgrim men took up weapons and marched to Corbitant's village to retrieve Squanto. When they reached the settlement, Corbitant was nowhere to be found, and Squanto was there, safe. The Pilgrims picked up their friend, and, to make their point clear, fired two shots of their guns into the air, frightening the inhabitants. Soon, Squanto was back in Plymouth.

Another challenge to the Pilgrims came in 1622, when a messenger from a chief of the Narragansetts, Canonicus, delivered a rattlesnake skin stuffed with arrows to the Pilgrims at Plymouth. Squanto explained to the Englishmen that the skin was a challenge to war. Not put off by the threat, William Bradford answered the challenge by filling the snakeskin with gunpowder and bullets and sending it back to Canonicus. This was a frightening answer to the Narragansetts, and the snakeskin was returned to Plymouth. There would be no fight between the Narragansetts and the Pilgrims, after all.

Squanto helped the English colonists in other ways as well. It was Squanto who taught the Pilgrims how to live off the bounty of the New England landscape. He instructed them how to plant

Indian corn and where to fish. Squanto helped the Pilgrims to plant 20 acres of Indian corn on a nearby hill. These fields required the labor of 21 men and 6 boys. At least one modern historian has calculated that these Pilgrim farmers dug, using a hoe or a mattock (a digging tool), 100,000 holes to plant corn seed in. Each hole also included "two or three alewives," (a type of small fish)[42] that were caught in a stream located at the bottom of the hill. It is estimated that the Pilgrims hauled 40 tons of fish up the hill to fertilize their corn mounds.

A TOWN TAKES SHAPE

By the summer of 1621, Plymouth was beginning to look like a small English village in exile. It is not clear exactly what the settlement site looked like, but the Pilgrims did write about it, including Bradford. The site was located on a small plateau of land, set back about 30 feet above the harbor and slanting back on the high ground the Pilgrims called Fort Hill. The hill was 165 feet high. The main street, which the settlers called "The Street," and which is Leyden Street today, ran to Fort Hill. As one walked down The Street from the harbor, the first building was the common house on the left side. Then, there were the family lots assigned to the leaders, including Brown, Goodman, and Brewster. On the right were the lots handed out to Fuller, Howland, and Hopkins. Another street connected to The Street at a right angle. Additional family lots lined this second street, including those of Billington, Allerton, Cook, and Winslow on the left, and Bradford, Standish, and Alden on the right. On these city lots sat seven log houses with thatched roofs.

Those Pilgrims who survived the difficulties of their first winter in the New World found themselves in much better condition by the fall of 1621. The harvest was abundant that autumn, the houses and buildings at Plymouth were up and complete, and the 51 English residents in good health. All these blessings called for a special recognition of God's Providence. Following the harvest, the Pilgrims celebrated with a feast of sorts. This, of course, is the origin of the modern holiday known as Thanksgiving.

Pilgrim leader Edward Winslow described this special day:

THE PILGRIMS' FIRST THANKSGIVING AND BEYOND

There is possibly no more enduring image from American history than that of the Pilgrims sitting down to their first Thanksgiving in the fall of 1621. It has become an American tradition, a special holiday that brings family members together to share a meal and spend time together.

But how similar is today's Thanksgiving to the event celebrated by the Pilgrims? Some facts are known. The fall meal lasted for three days, and included wild fowl, deer, and hasty pudding (cornmeal mush). Among the "fowl" may have been turkey, not stuffed, but roasted. There may also have been pumpkin in one form or another. (Both are almost always part of any modern-day Thanksgiving meal.) The other "fowl" could have included duck, geese, and even swans. Rounds of brandy and schnapps were also probably part of the meal. Among the foods enjoyed at today's Thanksgiving meals that the Pilgrims would not have had include sweet potatoes (they did not exist yet in New England), corn on the cob (Indian corn was only good for making cornmeal), and cranberry sauce (cranberries grew nearby, but sugar was not available).

When, exactly, the Pilgrims celebrated their 1621 Thanksgiving is a mystery. It would have fallen somewhere between September 21 and November 9, but the most likely date is in early October.

The Pilgrims' Thanksgiving in 1621 was an outdoor affair. There were simply too many people, including more than 50 colonists and more than 90 Wampanoag men (including Massasoit), to have fit everyone into one of the buildings at Plymouth. The day not only included an abundant meal, but games and activities. According to one Pilgrim record, following the meal, the Englishmen drilled with their weapons, while others engaged in outdoor games and the Wampanoags sang and danced.

While the 1621 event is remembered and repeated as a tradition today, it was a unique event for the Pilgrims. They did not repeat their Thanksgiving day celebrations the following year or any other year afterward. Today's Thanksgiving became a modern tradition through a series of historical events

Our harvest being gotten in, our governor sent four men on fowling [hunting], that so we might after a special manner rejoice together after we had gathered the fruit of our labors. The four in one day killed as much fowl as, with a little help beside, served the company almost a week. At which time,

that occurred long after the Pilgrims. Various early American presidents, including George Washington, declared one-time Thanksgiving holidays. President Abraham Lincoln issued his 1863 Thanksgiving Proclamation, making Thanksgiving a national holiday. Lincoln probably chose the date (the last Thursday in November) based on when the Pilgrims landed at Plymouth (November 21 on the modern calendar). It was President Franklin Roosevelt who chose Thanksgiving as the fourth Thursday of November, the date celebrated today.

In the fall of 1621, the Pilgrims and the Wampanoags celebrated the first Thanksgiving. However, the celebration did not become an annual affair until President Abraham Lincoln declared it a national holiday in 1863.

amongst other recreations, we exercised our arms. Many of the Indians coming amongst us, and among the rest their greatest King Massasoit, with some ninety men, whom for three days we entertained and feasted, and they went out and killed five deer, which they brought to the plantation and bestowed on our governor, and upon the captain and others. And although it be not always so plentiful as it was this time with us, yet by the goodness of God, we are so far from want.[43]

MAINTAINING PEACE

Peace with the local Native Americans remained an important goal to the Pilgrims during these early settlement years. They worked hard to maintain good relations with their neighbors. They did not train for war and instead relied on the skills of their only professional soldier, Captain Miles Standish. Squanto, living on a small plot of land in the Pilgrim settlement, served as a bridge between the English and the Native Americans. He was able to help maintain the peace until he died in 1622.

The Pilgrims and the local tribes of the region were able to avoid a general conflict through the first two years of their colony. Then, in 1623, fighting did take place. That year, Massasoit convinced the Pilgrim leader, Captain Miles Standish, to attack the Wampanoags' former allies, the Massachusetts, who lived north of Plymouth. When Standish did so, he returned with the head of the tribe's sachem and placed it on a pike outside the settlement's entrance. Even their allies, the Wampanoags, soon understood they would have to keep a close watch on the English. They began calling the Pilgrims *wotowquenange*, which translates as "cutthroats."

7

A Place in the Wilderness

The settlers of Plymouth Colony struggled during these early years to carve a settlement out of the harsh New England landscape. There had been those who wondered if the Pilgrims would be able to survive the challenges they faced living in the hostile frontier of North America. The Pilgrims had reached New England heavily in debt. The religious refugees who had abandoned England worked with their hands tending their gardens and fields, where they sowed corn and grain. They labored in the local forests cutting trees and sawing planks of lumber, backbreaking, but rewarding work. They traded with the local Native Americans for furs, a valuable commodity, which they sold in England. The year 1627 marked the end of their first seven years in New England, and their work was starting to show significant results. By then, they had built a town and were masters of their own lands and fields and trading posts. While that first winter of 1620–21 had been harsh and deadly, it had been their worst. The Pilgrim settlers would no longer have to worry about food, shelter, or clothing. Through hard work and perseverance, the colony not only managed to survive, but to prosper.

Even before these successes, the *Mayflower* Pilgrims were soon joined by others. The *Mayflower* had delivered 102 English persons to New England. Another 35 joined them in 1621 with the arrival of another ship, the *Fortune*. Sixty arrived on the *Anne* and the *Little James* in 1623. These new settlers put the total number to migrate to America between 1620 and 1623 at nearly 200. Of that number, 52 had died during the first winter at Plymouth. However, during the six years between 1621 and 1627, only six died! The Pilgrims had grown accustomed to the rigors of New England life. As for Plymouth in 1627, the population had grown by about 50 percent. Among the 156 residents, there were 57 men, 29 women, 34 boys, and 36 girls. There were still 42 who had come over on the *Mayflower*. An inventory of their livestock included four cows they owned in common, seven young heifers, four young bulls, eighteen goats, and a host of pigs and poultry. After 1627, additional colonists reached Plymouth, including 35 who arrived in August 1629, onboard the *Mayflower*. The next May, 60 more arrived in Plymouth onboard the *Handmaid*. It was a grand reunion of sorts. Forty-seven of these colonists were from the old Leyden congregation. By 1627, Plymouth and its outlying communities were solidly established, which would lead to further colonization of New England beginning a few years later.

FURTHER GROWTH IN NEW ENGLAND

Within 10 years of the founding of the Pilgrim Colony at Plymouth by the Separatists, along with other colonists the Puritans called "strangers," the colony witnessed a great wave of new settlers who found their way to New England. With each new group of arrivals, life in the colony changed dramatically.

By the mid-1620s, England experienced the rise of a new monarch to the throne—Charles I. He was not sympathetic to the Puritans in England, just as his father, James I, had not been. Many members of Parliament were Puritans who were prepared to challenge the royal power of the English sovereign. This led King Charles to send agents out to persecute as many Puritans as possible. History was repeating itself, as royal representatives broke into Puritan meetinghouses, harassed their leaders, and arrested many. So, in 1629, John Winthrop, a Puritan lawyer, decided he and his fellow believers could find a better life in America. He organized a group of would-be Puritan emigrants who were eager to go to New England and establish new homes.

The previous year, the Council of New England, the ruling Puritan body in Plymouth, granted a group of Puritans a patent on some land located between the Merrimack and Charles rivers, north of Plymouth. It was John Winthrop's group that obtained the charter to set up a royal colony from King Charles in March 1629. The following year, 1630, the Massachusetts Bay Company was formed to establish a new colony for Puritans in America. It took its name from a local Indian tribe called the Massachusetts, which meant "near the great hill." The company organized recruitments to New England, and in March, 11 ships carrying more than 1,000 emigrants left for America. This was the largest group of settlers that had ever left Europe bound for America. The ships arrived in New England and landed on June 12, 1630, at a site they called Salem.

John Winthrop was the group's leader. After the arrival of the "Great Migration," he was appointed as the first governor of the Massachusetts Bay Colony. Despite the group's high hopes, however, they faced immediate disappointment when they landed. The organizers of the Massachusetts Bay Company had sent a small group of colonists ahead of the main

In 1630, John Winthrop, the first governor of the Massachusetts Bay Colony, arrived at Salem with more than 1,000 Puritan settlers (his fleet is depicted in this woodcut). The colony grew quickly, and by 1640, it boasted 16,000 residents.

migration group to help locate and prepare the site for the later arrivals. When the ships of the Great Migration arrived, they found one out of every four of the advance group had already died. This sent a shock through the newly arrived colonists, causing several to decide to leave even though they had only just arrived. In all, 200 of the new settlers decided to return to England rather than accept the risks involved in remaining in America. Even though a decade had passed since the landing of the Pilgrims at Plymouth, life in New England was still difficult.

As for Governor Winthrop, he knew that the key to his colony's ultimate survival rested in the delivery of much-needed supplies and food from England to Salem. With that in mind, he sent one of the 11 ships, the *Lyon*, back to England under his orders to retrieve supplies for the colony. But before the *Lyon* could return, 200 Puritan settlers died in the Massachusetts Bay Colony. Many of those died of the same type of malnutrition and vitamin deficiency that had plagued the first group of Pilgrims—scurvy. If only the *Lyon* had returned earlier than February 1631, for among its much-needed supplies was a cure for scurvy—a large quantity of lemons.

That first winter of 1630–31 proved to be difficult. But the settlers worked hard, building shelters. One of the first structures Winthrop ordered built was the Puritan meeting-house, for worship. Some help came to the Massachusetts immigrants from neighboring Plymouth. Despite shipments of supplies from England, the Puritans came to rely on local foods for their survival, such as clams, seafood, and Indian corn. The new colonists slowly became accustomed to life in New England.

Early on, Salem proved to be an inadequate location to support a large community, so Winthrop moved many of his people south to the site that was named Charlestown. But there, problems also arose. The water supply was inadequate to support the large group, so Winthrop moved them one more time, to a place nearby that was named Boston, after an English port of the same name. This location proved suitable and reliable, and Boston soon became the main town of the colony.

THE NEW ENGLAND WAY

As the decades of the 1600s passed, the English became an increasing presence in New England. With each new addition, the region became more settled and less risky for the next group of new arrivals. Between 1629 and 1643, 20,000 new English colonists reached the colonies of Plymouth, Salem, Massachusetts Bay, and other destinations along or near the Atlantic coast of modern-day Massachusetts. Boston became the center of it all, the beehive of colonization, as settlers moved out from there, fanning in all directions to a distance of 30 miles away. The pattern of settlement in New England became known as the "New England Way." To an extent, the pattern might resemble that of life in England itself. But there was a unique element about the New World settlements. The first step in establishing each site was to build houses, nearly all of which resembled those they had lived in back home in England. They were wooden dwellings, with a single room, the outer walls covered with clay daub mixed with animal dung. These "daub and wattle" homes were roofed with bundles of reeds or thatch and were similar to the homes built by other English colonists in places such as Jamestown.

In time, as the settlements the Puritans established became more prosperous, they built larger homes, often two-story models, with horizontal siding of overlapping clapboard. One such pattern was the well-known saltbox house of the 1600s, which was identifiable by roofs that were steeper on one side than the other (as a way of keeping heavy snows from accumulating). Such homes, especially those of the wealthier colonists, might include gables, with decorative window boxes that extended out from the saltbox's roof line.

By the second generation of Puritan settlement in New England, houses also included small windows and a front entry door centered on one side of the dwelling. Inside, the house's first floor had a centrally situated fireplace that was used to cook meals, as well as providing a source of warmth for the house. A staircase was positioned at the front entrance of the house for easy access to the second story. The first floor was typically divided into four equal-sized rooms, which included a sitting room (also called "the best room"), a front room similar to a modern-day living room, a kitchen and dining room (where the fireplace opened up), and a spare room that might provide a servant with a bedroom or that could be used for storage. There were windows, but they were generally small and few in

As settlements in the New England colonies became prosperous, saltbox houses, such as the one pictured here, became the norm. These two-story homes had steep roofs that kept snow from piling up over the long New England winter.

number (glass was expensive to import), causing the house's interior to be dark.

Upstairs, the house might be divided into two bedrooms. These rooms were often sparsely decorated with little furniture, each piece serving a specific functional purpose. This was true of nearly all the rooms. The kitchen might have no more furniture than a log wooden table where the entire family could sit down together and partake in a meal. (Younger children, however, were not provided a place at the table, but were expected to stand during each meal.) The kitchen utensils and food service were equally basic and essential. Most colonists in early New

England ate off inexpensive wooden bowls or platters, called trenchers, using wooden spoons. Forks were not commonly used even in England at that time. Other kitchen items might include pots, pans, butter churns, kettles, skillets, roasting spits, and an early model of a bread toaster: a wrought-iron rack that could be turned on a pivot to toast both sides of the bread.

These homes provided shelter and security to entire families. In New England, family life was one of the most important aspects of colonial living. Many of those who migrated to New England came as family units that might include not only a mother and father, and children (as many as five to eight!), but a grandmother and/or grandfather, as well. With this many children in New England, it should come as no surprise that schools were important to the Puritan colonists. By the second and third generations, these early New Englanders were living longer, had more children, and were healthier than those living in other seventeenth-century New World settlements.

GOVERNING NEW ENGLAND

When a new group of Puritan immigrants established the Massachusetts Bay Colony, only those who were members had the right to engage in governing the colony. But many of the company members were only investors who never intended to leave England. Their only interest in colonization was to make a profit from the efforts of others in America. This proved to be an unacceptable situation to the Puritan emigrants. These independent-minded colonists did not find it easy to accept leadership and instruction from those who rested comfortably in England. In August 1629, the company's stockholders agreed to either migrate to America and become an active part of the New England colony or sell their investment shares. This caused most of the investors to sell their stock. By December 1630, less than 1 percent (fewer than 20 of the 2,000 investors) of those with a stake in the Massachusetts Bay Company were still members of the joint-stock company.

This changed things in the Massachusetts Bay Colony. Leadership would not be centered 3,000 miles away in London. Those who chose to come to America and take up residence in the Massachusetts Bay Colony would have full control of how it would be governed. The change helped provide Massachusetts with a different kind of power base from the other English colonies along the Atlantic coast. Massachusetts residents became accustomed to making their own important decisions. They had not only left England to come to America, they had cut other important ties with their mother country.

In addition, local rule received a further boost when, in October 1630, more than 100 male colonists requested to be declared freemen, or members of the community with full rights. The Massachusetts Bay Company granted the men this important status, but only if they were Puritans. Those colonial settlers who were "strangers," outsiders to the Puritan faith, objected to this. They continued to demand the right to vote. As long as the number of freemen was limited only to those who were Puritans, the number of voters remained fairly small. Under the original charter, a General Court had been established, which included a governor and his deputy (also known as the lieutenant governor), a board of magistrates who advised the governor, and the members of the corporation—the freemen.

The General Court met four times each year. During the rest of the year, the governor, his deputy, and the board of magistrates governed the colony. The freemen elected these magistrates annually. But the freemen remained dissatisfied with this system. They had no direct voice in the decision-making processes of the colony. Their political power also was limited, because they lived so scattered from one another. They wanted a greater voice, one that reflected their true numbers.

To help remedy this problem, it became the tradition for each Puritan town and village to send two men, called deputies, to the General Court. These men would sit in on the meetings of the General Court. By 1644, an official split was recognized between the deputies and the assistants to the governor. The deputies met as a lower house of the legislature, while the governor and his assistants met as the upper house. What had developed throughout the 1630s and early 1640s was a unique system of New World government.

Changes in the corporate structure of the Massachusetts Bay Company led to expanded voting rights for those adult males called freemen. In addition, the split between the freemen deputies and the governor's assistants created a two-house legislature, or bicameral system of government. Today, the U.S. Congress is structured the same way as are the state legislatures of 49 of the 50 states. (Nebraska is the only state with a unicameral, or one-house, government.) Through these early colonial innovations, a form of representative democracy was established.

NEW ENGLAND EXPANSION

The establishment of the Massachusetts Bay Colony and other colonial settlements was the most important event that took place among the Puritans of New England between the years 1627 and 1657. As early as 1628, settlements were springing up in every direction from Plymouth like the spokes of a wagon wheel. New England became home to first hundreds, then thousands of people. As early as 1634, 4,000 English colonists were living in 20 towns and villages near Boston. In the surrounding fields, 1,500 head of cattle grazed on New World grasses, alongside 4,000 goats.

During the 12 years between 1628 and 1640, more immigrants arrived in New England, delivered by no fewer than 200

With its founding in 1636, Harvard College became the first institution of higher learning in the United States. Named after Puritan minister John Harvard, the school included just nine students in its inaugural class, but today has more than 18,000.

sailing ships. Along with them came thousands of cattle and other animals. Among these new immigrants, several were well educated—even university trained and graduated. By 1639, records indicate that at least 70 university graduates were counted among the English population living in New England. By then, the Puritans had established their own university near Boston. Harvard College was founded in 1636, "at a time when it is probable that at Plymouth children were still being taught by Elder Brewster and some of the women, and taught nothing beyond the [basics]."[44]

By 1640, the Massachusetts Bay Colony boasted a total population of 16,000 people. Towns were established along the

Connecticut River, around New Haven, and in central Massachusetts, far inland from the coast. Others were settling to the south in Providence, Rhode Island, and to the north in New Hampshire and Maine. So many English-speaking people were immigrating to New England, not to mention those born there, that they were far outstripping the numbers and influence of other North American populations, including the French, the Dutch, and the Native Americans combined. The result would redirect American history: "The English language, English law and institutions became paramount [most important] on the soil of North America."[45]

8

The Pilgrims' Legacy

The legacy of the Puritans in the New World would extend beyond the confines of such settlement sites as Plymouth and the Massachusetts Bay Colony. In fact, over time, additional colonies were founded by those who did not always agree with Puritan dogma. Even as the colonial government of Massachusetts helped establish the root of American democracy, the political system it developed was far from perfect. From the earliest days of the *Mayflower* reaching the waters of New England, the colonial founders—the Puritans who settled Plymouth and the Massachusetts Bay Colony—were driven by their religion as much as anything else. It was always considered important, even crucial, that the region's political leaders had to be members of the Puritan faith. While this system gave the Puritans a framework of support for their beliefs, it did not appeal to those who were not themselves members of that narrowly defined sect.

Governor Winthrop believed the Massachusetts Bay Colony had been established by Providence and God's will and that

In 1635, Roger Williams was banned from Massachusetts because he believed that government should not be involved in religious matters. The following year, he bought land from the Narragansett Indians in present-day Rhode Island and named his new settlement Providence.

the people who populated the colony should be prepared and willing to follow the will of His representatives—namely the Puritan elders and ministers. Typically, such leaders expected all Puritans to act, think, and believe the same way about the same things. The result was to be "a harmony between all members of like faith."[46] However, in practicality, some Puritans pursued different religious ideas from those of their brethren. Such individuals sometimes found themselves not only on the wrong side of their local congregation's leaders, but in opposition to the political powers, who were sometimes the same people.

PURITAN CHALLENGERS

One such independent-minded Puritan was Roger Williams. He was a young minister who arrived in Massachusetts in 1631. He appears to have had his own ideas about faith. In fact, Williams was in many ways more conservative about his theology than many of his fellow Puritans. While some Puritans, such as John Winthrop, believed in the hope of eventually "purifying" the Church of England, Williams held no such expectation. Instead, he thought true believers should sever all ties with the English state church. Within two years after his arrival in New England, he was actively and publicly speaking against the king of England, Charles I.

Even though Governor Winthrop was Williams's friend, he came to believe that Williams posed a threat to the colony of Massachusetts Bay. By October 1635, the governor's assistants summoned Williams to explain himself. Before them, the controversial minister was penitent, appearing sorry for his outspoken ways. However, as soon as he returned to his home in Salem, he began speaking out, not only against the king, but against the Massachusetts Bay charter. (The king, after all, had issued the charter.)

Williams wasted little time announcing his belief that the elected leaders of the Massachusetts Bay Colony did not have the right to make laws regarding how one practiced his or her religion. Such a bold statement brought about a response from the Massachusetts Bay Colony's leaders who decided to vote against Williams. The result was that the fiery minister was banished from the colony. In 1636, Williams made his way out of the colony to Narragansett Bay, where he lived with the local Native Americans. In time, Williams bought land from the natives and founded the town of Providence. Through his later efforts, the colony of Rhode Island was established.

The Puritan leaders faced another problem during the same years they were being challenged by Williams. This time the problem was a woman named Anne Hutchinson. She arrived in the colony with her husband in 1634. Hutchinson soon became well known for her regular religious discussion groups. These meetings were usually held in her home. The topic was usually the content of the previous Sunday's public sermon. A very devout woman, she came to criticize some Boston ministers for their lack of piety.

Such criticism of Puritan leaders by a woman led the General Court to call Hutchinson to make an accounting of her accusations. Standing before the Puritan men of the General Court in November 1637, Hutchinson argued well against their accusations that she had stepped out of line as a Puritan woman and wife. But when she claimed that she had received a direct revelation from God, her words sealed her fate. The General Court ordered her and her family banished from the colony. In May 1638, "Mistress Anne" and her family moved to join Roger Williams on Narragansett Bay. A few years later, Hutchinson and others established a new community at Westchester. Sadly, she and members of her family were killed in a raid by Native Americans.

NEW ENGLAND COLONIAL PATTERN

Two forces came into conflict in colonial New England. There was constant pressure for colonists to conform to the religious standards set by the Puritan leaders of Plymouth and the

Massachusetts Bay Colony. Add to this the ever-increasing number of new arrivals in New England, and the result was a movement to establish additional colonies, such as Connecticut, Rhode Island, and New Hampshire, as well as a variety of scattered settlements within what is now Massachusetts.

The pattern typically began with the founding of a settlement. Land distribution in the New England colonies was, from the arrival of the *Mayflower*, different from the pattern established in other colonies along the Atlantic coast, such as Virginia and Maryland. In this region, land was doled out through the headright system, which provided individuals 50 acres of land once they paid their ship passage and arrived in the New World. But, in New England, the model relied on people living communally in close proximity to one another and holding land together.

The point of such a system was to encourage town settle ment and growth. Called the town system, it began in the Massachusetts Bay Colony and spread to other colonies. In design, it could not have been more simple. A group of colonizing families banded together to establish a new town. But first they had to approach the General Court to grant them permission. The court would examine the prospective settlers to see first if they were good, practicing Puritans. Once they cleared the colonists, the court checked on a site to ensure it could support the group. An adequate water source was important, the soil had to be good for farming, and other questions, such as defense of the location, had to be considered.

Once the General Court decided a given site was acceptable, it would grant the land to the would-be settlers. Most such land grants measured six miles square. Town officials, known as proprietors, were then selected. It was up to the proprietors to divide up the property to the various families in the group. Plans were soon made to build a community church building and locate a minister for the new flock. Often, a grassy meadow was selected as the center of the town, known as the village green. The green was usually located in the middle of the new community. Private family dwellings, as well as a school, Puritan meetinghouse, and blacksmith shop were often the first buildings erected in the new settlement site. A gristmill was built on a nearby stream, where the colonists' corn was ground into meal.

The town meetinghouse was not just used for Puritan worship services. It was also used as a meeting hall for the townsmen to assemble to discuss town business and other re-lated issues. During such meetings, the freemen selected those they wished to represent them at the General Court in Boston. Such meetings were still another form of early democracy in colonial America. Voting was limited to male landowners, but it provided another seed for the development of representa-tive government.

Such towns also established schools for their children. A 1647 Massachusetts law required every Puritan town with a population of 50 families to establish a school for its children. Towns numbering 100 families were to establish "grammar" school for older boys where they were taught Latin as a prepa-ration for college. This emphasis on schooling in New England produced the highest literacy rate of any of the colonies—a rate even higher than in most of Europe. As important as schooling was for Puritan boys, it was not emphasized for Puritan girls. Educating women was not valued by the Puritans at Plymouth. Among the daughters of the colony's leaders, most could not read. Even Governor Bradford's wife was illiterate! Schooling for girls came much later. An attempt to establish a school for girls in Plymouth was opposed even as late as 1793. One reason given: It might teach young girls who later became wives how to correct their husbands' spelling errors.

ESTABLISHING NEW COLONIES

As Puritans began fanning out across New England, they established new colonies. But a new colony could not be established by just anyone at any time of his choosing. A colony required a charter from the English monarch, which sometimes took years. By the time such a land grant became official, colonists were already living in the new colony. The colony of Rhode Island was first populated by those who, for a variety of reasons, left the Massachusetts Bay Colony. The dissident Roger Williams and the banished Anne Hutchinson were among the first. Williams helped establish the settlement at Providence. The modern-day city of Portsmouth was settled in 1638 by 18 people from the Massachusetts Bay Colony, and their leader was a close friend of Anne Hutchinson.

In 1643, Roger Williams went to England to obtain a charter from King Charles I, but things did not go according to plan. While Williams was in England, Charles faced a civil war, led by the Puritans, which ended with the king's beheading and the rise to power of the Puritans. Naturally, Williams received his land charter in 1644 from his fellow believers in Parliament. Four years later, the towns of Providence and Portsmouth, as well as new settlements at Newport and Warwick, banded together and formed a separate colony called Rhode Island.

Other dissatisfied residents of Massachusetts had already moved into the rich, fertile valley of the Connecticut River. In 1633, some Plymouth residents established a settlement they called Windsor, situated on the river, about 40 miles from Long Island Sound. Others followed shortly. Three years later, additional colonists came from the Massachusetts Bay Colony and settled in Windsor, Wethersfield, and Hartford, all located close to one another on the Connecticut River. By 1637, these townspeople formed a government that included a governor, assistants, and nine representatives, three from each town. Their

In 1644, shortly after the Puritans had taken control of the government during the English Civil War, Roger Williams received a charter to establish the colony of Rhode Island. Unlike most other colonies' charters, Rhode Island's charter guaranteed religious freedom, even for Catholics and Jews.

written constitution was called the Fundamental Orders, which was adopted in 1639. This document gave all men the right to vote, regardless of church membership. The new colony was named for the Connecticut River. Although Connecticut grew and new settlements were built, including coastal New Haven, the colony did not receive a charter until 1662.

Additional colonists established settlements north of the Massachusetts Bay Colony, as well. One early resident of the colony that became New Hampshire was Anne Hutchinson's brother-in-law, who established a settlement known as Exeter. Still others built the town of Hampton. Many early New Hampshire settlers were dissidents. By 1679, King Charles II granted the colony of New Hampshire its own charter.

THE PEQUOT WAR AND KING PHILIP'S WAR

As more and more colonists reached New England, their presence placed new and greater strains on the relations between the English settlers and the Native Americans of the region. Although the Puritans and the New England Indian tribes kept the peace through the early years, they would later go to war with one another more than once. In 1636, the colonists fought the Pequot tribe after they accused their warriors of killing a Boston trader. However, the Pequots had nothing to do with his death. The Narragansetts joined the colonists in fighting the Pequots. The resulting Pequot War brought on a massacre at their main village, including the deaths of women and children. Many other Pequots were either killed or taken into slavery.

A generation later, another war broke out in New England. The year was 1671 and the Plymouth leaders forced the Wampanoags to accept English authority over their traditional lands. This humiliating decision stirred the Wampanoags against the Puritans. A sachem named Metacom (also known as King Philip), the son of Massasoit, led his people against the English, shattering the peace that had existed between the English and Massasoit's people for a half-century. Soon, other tribes joined the Wampanoags. The region surrounding the Puritan settlements was soon dark with blood.

King Philip's War dragged on. During those months, Metacom and his warriors rampaged throughout the region of the Puritan settlements, setting homes on fire, burning Puritan

During King Philip's War (1675–1676), many colonial settlements in southern New England were attacked by local Native American groups. One of the first settlements attacked during the war was the central Massachusetts town of Brookfield, which was burned to the ground and not rebuilt until 11 years later.

fields and corncribs, and killing Englishmen. By the summer of 1676, colonial militia forces had driven most of the Native Americans into hiding. When Metacom himself was killed (he was shot by a Native American guide working for the English), he was decapitated and his body hacked into pieces. By the time the war ended, about 50 percent of the Native Americans living in New England had been either killed or had fled the region.

NEW ENGLAND'S SECOND CENTURY

Despite their resistance, the Native Americans of New England were fighting a relentless tide of colonization through much of the seventeenth century. The colonists had come to America searching for new lives, and they stood their ground against all hardships. Through hard work, determination, and religious faith, the Puritans managed to successfully establish themselves in New England. While those first arrivals, including the Pilgrims in 1620 and the Puritan founders of the Massachusetts Bay Colony in the 1630s, had struggled to create an economy based on the exportation of furs, fish, and lumber, these same colonies would, in time, develop expansive economic systems that were highly structured and diversified.

Coastal cities such as Boston and Salem in Massachusetts, and Newport in Rhode Island, had, by 1750, developed their economies to include merchandising, banking, shipbuilding, and shipping. As coastal communities, shipping had always been important to colonial life in New England. As early as the 1660s, New England shipping to the West Indies had begun to develop as an important aspect of the New England economy. By the 1700s, more than half the annual value of New England's shipping exports were bound for the West Indies. These ships carried a list of typical items produced in New England, including dried fish, livestock, wood products, whale products such as oil and spermaceti (a waxy substance found in the whale's head that made superb candles), and cereal grains. Nearly all of the last three items that were exported by the New England colonies went to the West Indies.

Although the populations of many New England towns reached their highest levels in the 1600s, many declined in the early 1700s; however, these towns still provided markets for the consumer goods produced by New England craftspeople. While many a pioneer colonist had brought few manufactured items to the New World, the established colonists wanted more consumer goods to make life easier and their work more productive. Such things as furniture, clothing, and tableware saw an increase in demand with each passing decade of the 1700s.

Farming had always been an important part of the New England economy, and it remained so in the 1700s. But more and more farmers found themselves going into debt in the eighteenth century, in part because they bought goods on credit. They needed more land for their farms, but little new land was available at that time. New farms were established primarily in western Massachusetts, to the north in modern-day Maine, and west of New Hampshire, in the Vermont territory.

THE FATE OF PLYMOUTH

Throughout the 1600s, the region of New England became colonized and settled. Because of the success of the first arrivals on the *Mayflower*, others were lured to stake their claim in the New World. Entire communities of English men and women uprooted themselves from their homes in England and made their way across the Atlantic, settling in villages and towns that had already been established or founding their own. This mass migration helped establish New England as a viable new world for English settlers. These communities grew at an astonishing rate.

The Pilgrims of Plymouth had started it all, and some of these colonists lived to see the tremendous effects of the seed they had helped plant in New England. But Plymouth was the exception in ways other than having been the first Puritan settlement along the Massachusetts coast. While other settlements and colonies grew quickly, Plymouth did not. Through the years, this first community experienced "slow, natural growth of [its] population."[47] While its first generation was made up of immigrants who had sought religious freedom, its second generation was born in the New World. Few others had joined their numbers over the years. Why did Plymouth's population not expand significantly through the 1600s?

One reason is that the location of Plymouth was not the best. The site the Pilgrims chose to settle on served them in 1621, but the site "occupied no strategic position for trading, for agriculture, or for communication."[48] The Pilgrims had chosen Plymouth without much thought to the future. Their main concern had been to create a world where they would be left alone. This might also explain why these religious settlers never chose to move their settlement, even when the disadvantages of Plymouth might have become obvious. As long as the population of Plymouth remained small, the colony's fields were adequate, even though there was much better land elsewhere. Plymouth harbor was deep enough for their small sailing ships, those weighing 30 to 80 tons. The Pilgrims never anticipated needing a deeper harbor. But it was too shallow for larger vessels that would come later and too small ever to become a major port. Plymouth, in the minds of the Pilgrims who had founded it, would always remain small, limited in population. For the first generation, that was just fine with them.

Some of the original Pilgrim party did come to realize that the Plymouth site was too limited. Miles Standish and John Alden knew it as early as 1631 and chose to move to another location, Duxbury, which had more fertile soil for farming. Even William Brewster followed them soon thereafter. As more and more people chose to leave Plymouth, the General Court proclaimed that "Plymouth should always be the seat

(continues on page 98)

CONNECTING WITH AMERICA'S PURITAN PAST

Today, thousands of tourists visit the living history complex at Plimoth Plantation in Massachusetts. Visitors may see re-creations of Pilgrim houses and other buildings, as well as a floating replica of the *Mayflower*. While these re-creations help give history buffs a feel and view for what life may have been like for the Pilgrims, they are only re-creations. But tourists to Plymouth may get a firsthand look at items actually connected to the Plymouth Colony by visiting the Pilgrim Hall Museum.

The museum is the place to see important collections that date back to the Pilgrims themselves. Situated along Court Street in Plymouth, the museum is home to a large display of historical artifacts, including household and personal items belonging to and dating to the time of the Pilgrims in the New World. Among its most important holdings are the books and paper materials, including the original text of the Mayflower Compact of 1620, signed by the adult males onboard the ship that delivered the Pilgrims to America. In addition, the museum houses such documents as personal inventories and the wills of various Pilgrims, including John Alden, William Bradford, William Brewster, John Winslow, and dozens of others. There are Native American documents as well, including the text of the treaty the English signed with Massasoit.

Perhaps the most intriguing items in the museum's collection are the various pieces of furniture, some associated with several of the colony's most important members. One of the oldest is the "Brewster Chest," a 30-inch-high chest fashioned out of Norway pine. It is thought that William Brewster had come into possession of the chest in Holland and brought it to England onboard the *Speedwell* and to New England onboard the *Mayflower*. The museum collection includes the "Thomas Prence Chair." Prence was elected governor of the Plymouth Colony in 1634. There is the "Miles Standish Chest," an oaken chest typical of Plymouth furniture of the seventeenth century. (This is not the same chest that was used as a writing desk onboard the *Mayflower* when the Pilgrim leaders wrote the Mayflower Compact.)

Since the 1830s, Pilgrim Hall has been the home to the "Brewster Chair," which was donated by the Brewster family. The chair is alleged to have belonged to William Brewster, who served as the Plymouth Colony's spiritual leader. The chair may have been built by a craftsman named John Eddy,

Today, visitors can tour the Plimoth Plantation in Plymouth, Massachusetts. The plantation includes a replica of the settlement as it appeared in
1627, along with a Wampanoag homesite, and a full-scale replica of the
Mayflower.

who migrated to Plymouth from Kent in 1630. The chair is one of the earliest
built in America. Another important chair in the Pilgrim Hall collection is the
"Bradford Chair," alleged to have been built in Plymouth and owned by Governor Bradford. In 1657, the year of Bradford's death, a household inventory
included two "great wooden chairs" in the family parlor.*

The chair was passed down through the Bradford family and its de-
scendants over the centuries until it was donated to the museum in 1953
by the Hedge family. (In 1921, President Warren Harding sat in the Bradford Chair during the three hundredth anniversary of the founding of
Plymouth Colony.) Today, the chair remains an important symbol of the
Pilgrims' colonial efforts in America. In 1995, Supreme Court Justice David
Souter sat in a replica of the Bradford Chair at the three hundred seventy-
fifth anniversary of the arrival of the Pilgrims in New England. During that
celebration, Justice Souter swore in 175 newly naturalized American citizens while sitting in the Bradford Chair replica.

---

* Available online at *www.pilgrimhall.org/brachair.html*

(continued from page 95)

of Government and that the Governor should reside there."[49] This, however, did not stop others from leaving Plymouth. By 1644, the tide had turned, and the majority of the Pilgrim settlers chose to pack up and leave Plymouth and move to the settlement site at Nauset, located on the great flexing arm beyond Cape Cod Bay. As for Governor Bradford, he chose to remain at Plymouth and lived out the rest of his life there. Several others chose to remain with him.

The fate of Plymouth was a sad one, as the original community of English settlers in New England became a forgotten village. It was a sadness that Bradford himself noted by penning a poem in 1654, "A Word to Plymouth." Its words are telling, its sentiment melancholy:

O Poor Plymouth, how dost thou moan,
Thy children are all from thee gone,
And left thou art in widow's state,
Poor, helpless, sad and desolate.[50]

Despite this sad reality and end for Plymouth (the colony was absorbed into the larger Massachusetts Bay Colony in 1691), history would never forget the contributions made by those who settled there in 1620. The Pilgrims had risked everything, had thrown caution toward a westward wind of discovery, and crammed themselves into a ship called the *Mayflower* to reach distant shores and build a new place on the frontier of New England, one where they could find peace and rediscover their faith, even while marking a trail for those whose ships would follow on that same wind.

Chronology

1534	King Henry VIII separates the church in England from the Catholic Church.
1563	Queen Elizabeth I, daughter of Henry VIII, calls a meeting of churchmen to consider a list of 39 changes for the Church of England to ensure it would remain Protestant.
1606	Scrooby congregation of Brownists decide to separate from the Church of England, establishing the Plymouth (England) Church.
Summer 1607	Separatist leader William Brewster is prepared to move his congregation from England.
September 1607	Scrooby members prepare to leave England for Holland.
November 1607	Leaders of the Scrooby congregation, including William Brewster, are summoned before Anglican officials in York; Brewster escapes arrest; his congregation's attempt to leave England fails.
Spring 1608	Scrooby members make a second attempt to leave England for Holland; after some problems with authorities, several have succeeded.
August 1608	Last members of the Scrooby congregation to leave England have arrived in Holland.
February 1609	Puritans deliver a letter to city authorities in Leyden, Holland, requesting permission to move to the city.
Winter 1616–1617	First serious discussions among the Leyden Puritans about leaving Holland.
Summer 1617	Puritan leaders John Carver and Robert Cushman meet with members of the Virginia Company to discuss colonization in America.

1617–1619 Smallpox epidemic ravages the Indian tribes of New England, dramatically reducing the population.

Early Spring 1620 Puritans at Leyden gain permission to colonize in America; they form a partnership with a group of London merchants.

July 1620 Puritans set out for Delftshaven, to take passage on the *Speedwell*.

September 1620 The *Mayflower* and the *Speedwell* set sail from Plymouth, England, with a group of Puritans headed to America.

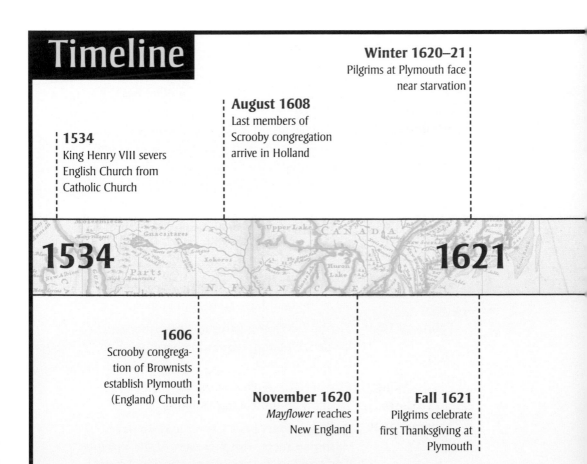

Timeline

1534
King Henry VIII severs English Church from Catholic Church

August 1608
Last members of Scrooby congregation arrive in Holland

Winter 1620–21
Pilgrims at Plymouth face near starvation

1534

1621

1606
Scrooby congregation of Brownists establish Plymouth (England) Church

November 1620
Mayflower reaches New England

Fall 1621
Pilgrims celebrate first Thanksgiving at Plymouth

November 1620	The *Speedwell* begins to leak and returns to England; the *Mayflower* reaches New England; within days of landing at Cape Cod, the adult males onboard sign the *Mayflower Compact*.
December 1620	Pilgrims move from Cape Cod to Plymouth.
Winter 1620–1621	The Pilgrims at Plymouth face near starvation and disease, which kills half their number.
January 1621	The men of the colony have constructed a Puritan meetinghouse.

1640
Population of Massachusetts Bay Colony reaches 16,000

1630
Massachusetts Bay Company is formed to colonize in America

1691
Plymouth Colony absorbed into Massachusetts Bay Colony

1675–76
King Philip's War fought

1630

1691

1629–1643
20,000 new English colonists reach Plymouth, Salem, the Massachusetts Bay Colony, and other Massachusetts sites

1644
Majority of Puritan residents at Plymouth pack up and move to Nauset

Summer 1621 The Plymouth group has braved its first winter and will soon bring in a bountiful harvest.

Fall 1621 Pilgrims celebrate their first Thanksgiving at Plymouth; another ship, the *Fortune*, arrives with 35 new colonists.

1620–22 Squanto, a local Native American, lives close to the Plymouth settlement and teaches the men to fish and plant corn.

1623 Chief Massasoit convinces Captain Miles Standish to help in a war against a neighboring tribe, the Massachusetts; that same year, 60 new colonists arrive at Plymouth on the *Anne* and the *Little James*.

1627 Puritans at Plymouth have paid off their debts to London merchants and the colony has become a success.

1629 John Winthrop organizes a new group of Puritan immigrants eager to come to America; Winthrop's group is granted a charter to colonize in New England in March.

1630 The Massachusetts Bay Company is formed to colonize in America; that March, 11 ships carrying 1,000 emigrants leave from England; they land in June at a site they call Salem.

1630–31 The first winter for the Massachusetts Bay Colony is difficult, leaving 200 colonists dead.

1629–43 Twenty thousand new English colonists reach the colonies of Plymouth, Salem, Massachusetts Bay, and other Massachusetts sites.

1636 Puritan dissident Roger Williams is banished from the Massachusetts Bay Colony and finds his way to Narragansett Bay; that same year, the Pequot War is fought.

1637 Connecticut Colony's leaders frame the Fundamental Orders, giving every adult male the right to vote.

1638 General Court of the Massachusetts Bay
Colony banishes Anne Hutchinson and her
family; they join Williams at Narragansett;
that same year, 18 immigrants from the
Massachusetts Bay Colony found the
modern-day city of Portsmouth.

1640 Massachusetts Bay Colony boasts a population of 16,000 people.

1644 The majority of the Puritan residents at
Plymouth pack up and move to the settlement site at Nauset.

1647 A Massachusetts law is passed requiring every
Puritan town with a population of 50 families
to establish a school for its children.

1670s King Philip's War is fought; by the time
the war ends, half of New England's Native
American population has been killed or has
fled the region.

1691 Plymouth Colony is absorbed into the larger
Massachusetts Bay Colony.

Notes

Chapter 1

1. David Hawke, *The Colonial Experience* (Indianapolis: The Bobbs-Merrill Company, Inc., 1966), 124.
2. Ibid.
3. Edmund Janes Carpenter, *The Mayflower Pilgrims* (New York: The Abingdon Press, 1918), 31.
4. Ibid., 27.
5. Roland G. Usher, *The Pilgrims and Their History* (Williamstown, Mass.: Corner House Publishers, 1977), 19.
6. Ibid., 21.

Chapter 2

7. Peter Charles Hoffer, *The Brave New World: A History of Early America* (Boston: Houghton Mifflin Company, 2000), 179.
8. Usher, 23.
9. Ibid., 26.
10. Ibid., 27.
11. Ibid., 28.

Chapter 3

12. Ibid., 29.
13. Ibid.
14. Ibid., 31.
15. Ibid.
16. Ibid., 32.
17. Ibid.
18. Carpenter, 47.
19. Ibid., 50.
20. Ibid., 69.

Chapter 4

21. Usher, 45.
22. Ibid., 59.
23. Ibid., 63.
24. Mary Caroline Crawford, *In the Days of the Pilgrim Fathers* (Boston: Little, Brown, and Company, 1921), 54.
25. Carpenter, 74.
26. Usher, 65.
27. Ibid.
28. Crawford, 96.
29. Carpenter, 78.
30. Ibid.
31. Ibid., 79.

Chapter 5

32. Crawford, 100.
33. Ibid., 100–01.
34. Usher, 77.
35. Carpenter, 81.
36. Ibid., 90.

Chapter 6

37. Ibid., 78.
38. Ibid., 81.
39. Ibid.
40. Carpenter, 98–99.
41. Usher, 119.
42. Ibid., 91.
43. Available online at *www.pilgrims.net/plymouth/thanksgiving.htm*

Chapter 7

44. Usher, 172.
45. Ibid., 171.

Chapter 8

46. McNeese, 31.
47. Usher, 177.
48. Ibid., 179.
49. Ibid., 181.
50. Ibid., 182.

Bibliography

Carpenter, Edmund Janes. *The Mayflower Pilgrims.* New York: The
    Abingdon Press, 1918.

Crawford, Mary Caroline. *In the Days of the Pilgrim Fathers.* Boston:
    Little, Brown, and Company, 1921.

Davis, William T., ed., *Bradford's History of Plymouth Plantation,
    1606–1646.* New York: Barnes & Noble, 1959.

Hawke, David. *The Colonial Experience.* Indianapolis: The Bobbs-
    Merrill Company, 1966.

Hoffer, Peter Charles. *The Brave New World: A History of Early
    America.* Boston: Houghton Mifflin Company, 2000.

McNeese, Tim. *The American Colonies.* St. Louis: Milliken Publishing
    Company, 2002.

Morison, Samuel Eliot. *Builders of the Bay Colony.* Boston:
    Houghton Mifflin Company, 1958.

Stoddard, Francis R. *The Truth About the Pilgrims.* New York: Society
    of Mayflower Descendants in the State of New York, 1952.

Usher, Roland G. *The Pilgrims and Their History.* Williamstown,
    Mass.: Corner House Publishers, 1977.

Vaughn, Alden T. *New England Frontier: Puritans and Indians,
    1620–1675.* Boston: Little, Brown and Company, 1965.

Waller, George M., ed. *Puritanism in Early America.* Lexington,
    Mass.: D. C. Heath and Company, 1973.

Wertenbaker, Thomas Jefferson. *The Puritan Oligarchy: The
    Founding of American Civilization.* New York: Charles Scribner's
    Sons, 1947.

Willison, George F. *Saints and Strangers.* New York: Reynal &
    Hitchcock, 1945.

Further Reading

Bowen, Gary. *Stranded at Plimoth Plantation 1626.* New York: HarperCollins, 1994.

Bradford, William. *Homes in the Wilderness: A Pilgrim's Journal of Plymouth Plantation in 1620.* North Haven, Conn.: Shoe String, 1988.

Jehle, Paul. *Plymouth in the Words of Her Founders.* San Antonio, Tex.: The Vision Forum, 2003.

Philbrick, Nathaniel. *Mayflower: A Story of Courage, Community, and War.* New York: Viking, 2006.

Roop, Connie & Peter. *Pilgrim Voices: Our First Year in the New World.* New York: Walker, 1995.

Stratton, Eugene Aubrey. *Plymouth Colony: Its History and People.* Ancestry.com, 1997.

Web sites

The Pilgrims and America's First Thanksgiving
www.holidays.net/thanksgiving/pilgrims.htm

A Brief History of the Pilgrims
www.mayflowerfamilies.com/colonial_life/pilgrims.htm

Introduction to the Mayflower, the Pilgrims, and early Plymouth Colony
www.mayflowerhistory.com/History/history.php

Pilgrim Hall Museum
www.pilgrimhall.org

Gateway to Plymouth
www.pilgrims.net

Plymouth Plantation
www.plimoth.org/

Plymouth Rock Foundation
www.plymrock.org/who_were_the_pilgrims.htm

Picture Credits

2: Infobase Publishing

8: Library of Congress, [LC-USZC2-6373]

11: Bassetlaw Museum

13: Library of Congress, [LC-USZ61-625]

16: Library of Congress, [LC-USZ62-106321]

18: Getty Images

27: Library of Congress, [LC-USZ62-120401]

29: National Archives Canada

34: National Portrait Gallery, London

41: Photography Collection, Miriam and Ira D. Wallach Division of Art, Prints and Photographs, The New York Public Library, Astor, Lenox and Tilden Foundations

43: Library of Congress, [LC-D146-28072]

49: The Granger Collection, New York

53: Library of Congress, [LC-USZ62-120508]

58: Giraudon/Art Resource, NY

60: The Granger Collection, New York

64: The Granger Collection, New York

69: Library of Congress, [LC-USZC4-4961]

74: ©North Wind/North Wind Picture Archives

77: ©Philippa Lewis; Ediface/Corbis

81: I.N. Phelps Stokes Collection, Miriam and Ira D. Wallach Division of Art, Prints and Photographs, The New York Public Library, Astor, Lenox and Tilden Foundations

84: Emmet Collection, Miriam and Ira D. Wallach Division of Art, Prints and Photographs, The New York Public Library, Astor, Lenox and Tilden Foundations

90: Picture Collection, The Branch Libraries, The New York Public Library, Astor, Lenox and Tilden Foundations

92: © North Wind/North Wind Picture Archives

97: Associated Press, AP/Chitose Suzuki

Cover: Library of Congress, [LC-USZC4-4992]

Index

About the Author

Series editor and author **TIM MCNEESE** is associate professor of history at York College in York, Nebraska, where he is in his fifteenth year of college instruction. Professor McNeese earned an Associate of Arts degree from York College, a Bachelor of Arts in history and political science from Harding University, and a Master of Arts in history from Missouri State University. A prolific author of books for elementary, middle, high school, and college readers, McNeese has published more than 80 books and educational materials over the past 20 years, on everything from Picasso to landmark Supreme Court decisions. His writing has earned him a citation in the library reference work *Contemporary Authors*. In 2006, McNeese appeared on the History Channel program *Risk Takers/History Makers: John Wesley Powell and the Grand Canyon.*